PREFACE

1. Scope

This publication provides fundamental principles and guidance for planning, coordinating, and executing joint fire support across the range of military operations.

2. Purpose

This publication has been prepared under the direction of the Chairman of the Joint Chiefs of Staff. It sets forth joint doctrine to govern the activities and performance of the Armed Forces of the United States in joint operations and provides the doctrinal basis for interagency coordination and for US military involvement in multinational operations. It provides military guidance for the exercise of authority by combatant commanders and other joint force commanders (JFCs) and prescribes joint doctrine for operations, education, and training. It provides military guidance for use by the Armed Forces in preparing their appropriate plans. It is not the intent of this publication to restrict the authority of the JFC from organizing the force and executing the mission in a manner the JFC deems most appropriate to ensure unity of effort in the accomplishment of the overall objective.

3. Application

a. Joint doctrine established in this publication applies to the Joint Staff, commanders of combatant commands, subunified commands, joint task forces, subordinate components of these commands, and the Services.

b. The guidance in this publication is authoritative; as such, this doctrine will be followed except when, in the judgment of the commander, exceptional circumstances dictate otherwise. If conflicts arise between the contents of this publication and the contents of Service publications, this publication will take precedence unless the Chairman of the Joint Chiefs of Staff, normally in coordination with the other members of the Joint Chiefs of Staff, has provided more current and specific guidance. Commanders of forces operating as part of a multinational (alliance or coalition) military command should follow multinational doctrine and procedures ratified by the United States. For doctrine and procedures not ratified by the United States, commanders should evaluate and follow the multinational command's doctrine and procedures, where applicable and consistent with US laws, regulations, and doctrine.

For the Chairman of the Joint Chiefs of Staff:

LLOYD J. AUSTIN III
Lieutenant General, USA
Director, Joint Staff

Intentionally Blank

- **Consolidates Joint Publication (JP) 3-09.1,** *Joint Tactics, Techniques, and Procedures for Laser Designation Operations*, **into JP 3-09,** *Joint Fire Support*, **and cancels JP 3-09.1**

- **Clarifies what constitutes nonlethal fires and their purpose**

- **Expands the discussion of the joint fires element to explain the key functions and tasks it generally performs**

- **Updates the descriptions of the component fires command and control entities provided by the Services; to include new descriptions: forward air controller (air), tactical air controller (air), joint forward observer, joint tactical air controller and joint air component coordination element**

- **Adds paragraphs on the Advance Field Artillery Tactical Data System and Theater Battle Management Core Systems**

- **Eliminates detailed discussion on datums, coordinates systems, and area reference systems and references JP 2-03,** *Geospatial Intelligence Support to Joint Operations*, **for the source of this information**

- **Inserts new Joint Fire Support Assessment paragraph**

- **Adds an Airspace Coordinating Area subparagraph under Airspace Coordinating Measures paragraph in Appendix A**

- **Incorporated the JP 3-09.1 material into new Appendix C**

- **Modifies the definitions of counterfire, fires, schedule of fire, and supporting fire**

- **Creates new term and definition for concept of fires**

- **Removes from JP 1-02,** *Department of Defense Dictionary of Military and Associated Terms*, **the terms and definitions for: at my command, backscatter, call fire, call for fire, continuous illumination fire, direct support artillery, enlisted terminal attack controller, fire, fire, barrage (specify), fire capabilities chart, fire control, fire control radar, fire control system, fire coordination, fire for effect, fire message, fire mission, fire plan, firepower, firing chart, laser, laser footprint, laser linescan system, laser pulse duration, laser target designating system, laser-target/gun-target angle, laser target marker, laser** target making system, low angle, low angle fire, low angle loft bombing, offset lasing, pulse code, pulse repetition frequency, rate of fire, special operations terminal attack controler, spillover, and submunition

TABLE OF CONTENTS

PAGE

EXECUTIVE SUMMARY vii

CHAPTER I
JOINT FIRE SUPPORT OVERVIEW

- Introduction I-1
- Concept of Fires I-2
- Employment Considerations I-3
- Synchronization of Maneuver and Fires I-4
- Synchronizing and/or Integrating Maneuver and Interdiction I-5

CHAPTER II
JOINT FIRE SUPPORT COMMAND AND CONTROL

- Introduction II-1
- Joint Fire Support Command and Control II-1

CHAPTER III
JOINT FIRE SUPPORT PLANNING AND EXECUTION

- Introduction III-1
- Joint Fire Support Planning III-1
- Other Planning Considerations III-4
- Joint Fire Support Planning Process III-7
- Joint Fire Support Coordination III-12
- Joint Fire Support Assessment III-16
- Joint Fire Support and Force Capabilities III-17
- Joint Fire Support Coordination Measures and Reference Systems III-20
- Combat Identification III-20
- Mitigation of Collateral Damage III-21

APPENDIX

A Control and Coordination Measures A-1
B Joint Fire Support Operation Order Format B-1
C Laser-Guided Systems C-1
D References D-1
E Administrative Instructions E-1

GLOSSARY

    Part I   Abbreviations and Acronyms GL-1
    Part II Terms and Definitions GL-6

FIGURE

    II-1   Typical Joint Fires Element.. II-3
    III-1   Joint Fire Support Planning Process III-8
    A-1   Fire Support and Control Measures A-3
    A-2   Fire Support Coordination Line A-4
    A-3   Restrictive Fire Line, Fire Support Area, and Zone of Fire A-8
    C-1   Airborne and Ground Designator Advantages and Disadvantages.................C-6
    C-2   Example of Safety Zone, Acquisition Area, and Optimal Attack Zone...........C-8
    C-3   Hellfire Designator Exclusion Zone...C-9

EXECUTIVE SUMMARY
COMMANDER'S OVERVIEW

- **Describes the Joint Fire Support System**

- **Discusses Joint Fire Support Command and Control**

- **Delineates Joint Fire Support Planning and Execution**

Overview

Scope and Purpose

This publication **provides fundamental principles and guidance** for planning, coordinating, and executing joint fire support across the range of military operations. It sets forth joint doctrine to govern the activities and performance of the Armed Forces of the United States in joint operations and provides the doctrinal basis for interagency coordination and for US military involvement in multinational operations.

Introduction

Command and Control

The foundations of joint fire support are based on the elements of combat power, the principles of joint operations, and joint functions. The elements of combat power are combined to provide the basis for the generation of overwhelming firepower. The fire support system has its roots in the firepower element of combat power.

Joint Fire Support is Synchronized to Collectively Ensure Effective Fires.

Synchronized joint fire support requires the coordinated interaction of all of the elements of the fire support system, thorough and continuous planning, aggressive coordination, and vigorous execution. The fire support system includes the target acquisition, command and control (C2), and attack/delivery systems that must function collectively to ensure effective fires are delivered where and when the commander requires them.

Fires

Fires. Fires are defined as the use of weapon systems to create a specific lethal or nonlethal effect on a target. All fires are normally synchronized and integrated to achieve synergistic results. Fires can

---

be delivered by air, land, maritime, or special operations forces (SOF).

Joint Fires

Joint Fires

Joint Fires. Joint fires are defined as fires delivered during the employment of forces from two or more components in coordinated action to produce desired effects in support of a common objective.

Joint Fire Support

Joint Fire Support. Joint fire support is defined as joint fires that assist air, land, maritime, and SOF to move, maneuver, and control territory, populations, airspace, and key waters in support of the joint force commander's (JFC's) scheme of maneuver.

All Fires Should Support Joint Force Commander Objectives.

The concept of operations (CONOPS) describes how actions of the joint force components and supporting organizations will be integrated, synchronized, and phased to accomplish the mission, including potential branches and sequels. All fires should support the JFC's objectives. Some fires will support maneuver forces, and other fires are independent of maneuver and orient on creating specific effects.

Supported Commanders

The land and maritime force commanders are the supported commanders within the areas of operations (AOs) designated by the JFC. In coordination with the land and/or maritime force commander, those commanders designated by the JFC to execute theater and/or joint operations area (JOA)-wide functions have the latitude to plan and execute these JFC prioritized operations within land and maritime AOs. Any commander executing such a mission within a land or maritime AO must coordinate the operation to avoid adverse effects and fratricide. If those operations would have adverse impact within a land or maritime AO, the commander assigned to execute the JOA-wide functions must readjust the plan, resolve the issue with the land or maritime component commander, or consult with the JFC for resolution.

Preventive Measures for Limiting Fratricide

Commanders must identify and assess situations that increase the risk of fratricide. The primary preventive measures for limiting fratricide are comprehensive combat identification training, command emphasis, disciplined operations, fire support coordination measures, airspace coordination measures, close coordination among component commands, rehearsals, reliable and interoperable, battle tracking, effective procedures, and enhanced situational awareness.

Fundamental and Beneficial Effects of Teamwork

Combining joint fire support and maneuver relies on the fundamental and beneficial effects of teamwork, unity of effort, and synchronization of capabilities in time, space, and purpose. **Maneuver and joint fire support are complementary functions that are essential to achieving JFC objectives.** Joint fire support destroys, neutralizes, or suppresses enemy forces and disrupts enemy maneuver, both on the surface and in the air, which assists the maneuver of friendly forces.

Joint Fire Support Effects

Typically, the execution of joint fire support has an immediate or near term effect on the conduct of friendly operations.

Complementary Operations

Synchronizing and/or integrating interdiction and maneuver (air, land, and maritime) provides one of the most dynamic concepts available to the joint force. Interdiction and maneuver usually are not considered separate operations against a common enemy, but rather normally are considered complementary operations designed to achieve the military strategic and operational objectives.

Joint Fire Support Command and Control

Synchronization and Integration

The JFC, using systems that allow rapid response to changes as they occur, **is responsible for ensuring the synchronization and integration of joint fires.** The challenge for the JFC is to integrate and synchronize the wide range of capabilities at his disposal.

The Operations Directorate of a Joint Staff

The operations directorate of a joint staff (J-3) serves as the JFC's principal staff advisor for the coordination, integration, and synchronization of joint fire support with other major elements of operations such as C2, intelligence, movement and maneuver, protection, and sustainment. The J-3 recommends, coordinates, reviews, designates, and disseminates fire support coordination measures, maneuver control measures, and airspace coordinating measures as part of overall concept of the operations for joint fires and joint fire support.

Joint Fires Element

The JFC may approve the formation of a joint fires element (JFE) within the J-3. The JFE is an optional staff element comprised of representatives from the J-3, the components, and other elements of the JFC's staff, to include the intelligence directorate of a joint staff targeting staff, logistics directorate of a joint staff, plans directorate of a joint staff, and others as required. The JFE is an integrating staff element that synchronizes and coordinates fires planning and coordination on behalf of the JFC and should be physically located near the joint task force joint operations center, collocated with the information operations cell if possible. The JFE assists the J-3 in accomplishing responsibilities and tasks as a staff advisor to the JFC.

Joint Targeting and Coordination Boards

Typically JFCs organize joint targeting coordination boards (JTCB). The JFC has the responsibility to conduct planning, coordination, and deconfliction associated with joint targeting. When a JTCB is not established and the JFC decides not to delegate targeting oversight, the JFC may perform this task at the joint force headquarters. Typically, however, the JFC may establish a JTCB and appoints the deputy JFC or a component commander to chair it.

Unique Fire Support Command and Control Agencies

The land, air, maritime, and SOF components of a joint force all have unique fire support command and control agencies.

Joint Fire Support Planning and Execution

Integration in the Joint Planning Process

The key to effective integration of joint fire support is the thorough and continuous inclusion of all component fire support elements in the joint planning process, aggressive coordination efforts, and a vigorous execution of the plan.

Joint Fire Support Planners

Joint fire support planners and/or coordinators actively participate with other members of the staff to develop estimates, give the commander recommendations, develop the joint fire support portion of the CONOPS, and supervise the execution of the commander's decision. The effectiveness of their planning and coordination is predicated on the commander providing clear and precise guidance.

Purpose of Joint Fire Support Planning

The purpose of joint fire support planning is to optimize its employment by integrating and synchronizing joint fire support with the commander's maneuver plan. **During the planning phase, commanders develop a CONOPS, including the concept for fires. Commanders determine how to shape the operational environment with fires to assist maneuver and how to use maneuver to exploit the use of joint fire support.**

Four Basic Fire Support Tasks

Effective joint fire support depends on planning for the successful performance of the following four basic fire support tasks: **support forces in contact; support the CONOPS; synchronize joint fire support; and sustain joint fire support operations.**

Wartime Posture

When the instruments of national power (diplomatic, information, military, and economic) are unable to achieve national strategic objectives or protect national interests without force, the **US national leadership may decide to conduct a major operation involving large-scale combat, placing the United States in a wartime posture.** In such cases, the goal is to **prevail** against the enemy as quickly as possible, conclude hostilities, and establish conditions favorable to the United States, the host nation, and its multinational partners.

Crisis Response and Contingency Operations

Joint fire support employed in support of crisis response and contingency operations may be the same as those employed for major operations and campaigns but are normally more restrictive in their application.

Security Cooperation and Deterrence Operations

Lethal joint fire support employed in support of security cooperation and deterrence operations are normally the most restrictive in their application and may be limited to defensive fires only.

Multinational Operations

Fire support coordination in multinational operations demands special arrangements with multinational forces and local authorities. To maximize the fires of the multinational force and to minimize the possibility of fratricide, the multinational force commander and staff must become familiar with each nation's capabilities and limitations in munitions, digital capability, and training, to ensure that they develop good fire support coordination throughout the multinational force.

Joint Fire Support Planning

Joint fire support planning is accomplished utilizing both the targeting and joint fire support estimate processes. It is a continual and cyclical process of planning, synchronizing, and executing joint fires involving tactical, operational, and strategic considerations that also utilizes joint fire support command, control, and communications systems and architectures. Initiated during mission analysis and continuing through post-execution assessment, the joint fire support planning process includes the following steps: end state and the commander's objectives; target development and prioritization; capabilities analysis; commander's decision and force assignment; mission planning and force execution; and assessment.

Agencies Involved in Coordinating Joint Fire Support

Agencies involved in coordinating joint fire support employ several principles which are extensions of the four basic fire support tasks.

- **Plan early and continuously.**

- **Ensure continuous flow of targeting information.**

- **Consider the use of all lethal and/or nonlethal attack means.**

- Use the lowest echelon capable of furnishing effective support.

- Furnish the type of joint fire support requested.

- Use the most effective joint fire support means.

- Avoid unnecessary duplication.

- Coordinate airspace.

- Provide adequate support.

- Provide for rapid coordination.

- Protect the force.

- Analyze effectiveness.

- Provide for flexibility.

Joint Fire Support Coordination

Joint fire support coordination includes all efforts to deconflict attacks, avoid fratricide, reduce duplication of effort, and assist in shaping the operational environment. **Coordination procedures must be flexible and responsive to the ever changing dynamics of warfighting.**

Assessment

Assessment is a continuous process that measures progress of the joint force toward mission accomplishment. The JFC and component commanders assess the operational environment and the progress of operations, and compare them to their initial vision and intent.

Combat Identification

Combat identification is the process of attaining an accurate characterization of detected objects in the operational environment sufficient to support an engagement decision. Depending on the situation and the operational decisions that must be made, this characterization may be limited to "friend," "enemy," "neutral," or "unknown." In other situations, other characterizations may be required — including, but not limited to, class, type, nationality, and mission configuration.

Mensuration

Mensuration is the act of precisely measuring something and is commonly used in targeting to refer to the exact measurement (location) of a target's geographical coordinates. Point mensuration has always been an important part of targeting, since the points measured represent the desired points of impact for the munitions employed. As the accuracy of weapons delivery has improved, the importance of mensuration has grown in proportion and is a vital part of targeting.

Principle of Proportionality

Under the law of armed conflict, the principle of proportionality requires that the anticipated loss of civilian life and damage to civilian property incidental to attacks must not be excessive in relation to the concrete and direct military advantage expected to be gained. **Commanders therefore have the responsibility to attempt to minimize collateral damage to the greatest extent practicable.** Collateral damage estimation is an important step in the target development process. However, it should not preclude the inclusion of valid military targets on a target list.

CHAPTER I
JOINT FIRE SUPPORT OVERVIEW

"Joint fire support is defined as joint fires that assist air, land, maritime, and special operations forces to move, maneuver, and control territory, populations, airspace, and key waters."

Joint Publication 3-0, *Joint Operations*

1. Introduction

a. The joint force commander (JFC) and component commanders, with the assistance of their staffs, integrate and synchronize joint fire support in time, space, and purpose to increase the effectiveness of the joint force. The JFC organizes forces to accomplish the assigned mission based on the concept of operations (CONOPS). The organization should be sufficiently flexible to meet planned phases of contemplated operations and any development that may require a change in plan. The JFC establishes subordinate commands, assigns responsibilities, establishes or delegates appropriate command and support relationships, and establishes coordinating instructions for the component commanders. The JFC provides guidance to integrate components' capabilities and synchronize the execution of fires. Systems for delivering firepower may be limited, and there are competing priorities for employing these assets. Therefore, JFCs and their staffs carefully balance resources and requirements over the course of a joint operation to ensure the appropriate mix of forces and capabilities required to achieve the objective.

b. The foundations of joint fire support are based on the elements of combat power, the principles of joint operations, and joint functions. The elements of combat power are combined to provide the basis for the generation of overwhelming firepower. The fire support system has its roots in the firepower element of combat power. The principles of joint operations provide a set of time-tested guidelines for combining the elements of combat power and employing fire support. Joint functions are related capabilities and activities grouped together to help JFCs integrate, synchronize, and direct joint operations to include fires.

c. Synchronized joint fire support requires the coordinated interaction of all of the elements of the fire support system, thorough and continuous planning, aggressive coordination, and vigorous execution. The fire support system includes the target acquisition (TA), command and control (C2), and attack/delivery systems that must function collectively to ensure effective fires are delivered where and when the commander requires them.

(1) **Fires. Fires are defined as the use of weapon systems to create specific lethal or nonlethal effects on a target.** All fires are normally synchronized and integrated to achieve synergistic results. Fires can be delivered by air, land, maritime, or special operations forces (SOF).

(2) **Joint Fires. Joint fires are defined as fires delivered during the employment of forces from two or more components in coordinated action to produce desired effects in support of a common objective.** Joint fires are provided to assist forces (air, land, maritime, or SOF) in conducting operations across the range of military operations.

(3) **Joint Fire Support.** Joint fire support is defined as joint fires that assist air, land, maritime, and SOF to move, maneuver, and control territory, populations, airspace, and key waters in support of the JFC's scheme of maneuver. Integration and synchronization of joint fire support with the movement and maneuver of the supported force is essential. Prerequisites for effective joint fire support are interoperable systems, broad understanding of the differing strengths and limitations of each Service's capabilities and how they are applied, and clear agreement about how those capabilities will be integrated in any given operational setting.

2. **Concept of Fires**

The CONOPS describes how the actions of the joint force components and supporting organizations will be integrated, synchronized, and phased to accomplish the mission, including potential branches and sequels. The commander defines responsibilities by providing guidance to the staff and subordinate commanders. **Integral to the CONOPS is the concept of fires.** The concept of fires describes how lethal and nonlethal joint fires will be synchronized and integrated to support the JFC's operational objectives. The JFC determines the enemy's center of gravity (COG), associated critical factors, and decisive points and how the application of fires can assist in creating the desired effects to attain the objective. The JFC can also highlight the anticipated critical actions, times, and places that would serve as triggers for friendly action. The JFC determines the sequencing of key events and emphasizes the desired end state. Some fires will support maneuver forces and other fires are independent of maneuver and orient on creating specific effects. All fires should support the JFC's objectives. **The JFC provides guidance on his objectives and desired effects and priorities and what effects of fires should have on the enemy (e.g., deny, disrupt, delay, suppress, neutralize, destroy, or influence).** In addition, the JFC provides guidance on munitions usage and restrictions. The JFC also provides guidance on restricted targets and a no-strike list (NSL). Restricted targets are targets that have specific restrictions imposed upon them. Actions that exceed specified restrictions are prohibited until coordinated and approved by the establishing headquarters (HQ). This list also includes restricted targets directed by higher authorities. Items on an NSL are those objects or entities characterized as protected from the effects of military operations under the law of armed conflict, international law and/or rules of engagement (ROE). Additional considerations for an NSL could include conventions, or agreements, or damaging relations with the indigenous population. The JFC may also make available specific assets for operational area-wide employment, such as Army Tactical Missile Systems (ATACMSs), sensor-fuzed weapons, or Tomahawk land attack missiles (TLAMs), and nonlethal assets designed to enable or disable materiel, personnel, and networks.

3. Employment Considerations

a. **Complementary and Interdependent.** The JFC integrates diverse fires assets from air, land, maritime, SOF, and multinational forces. To maximize the effects of fires, complementary and interdependent actions are required. These actions include planning, target acquisition, execution, and assessment.

b. **Command and Control in Operational Areas.** The land and maritime force commanders are the supported commanders within the areas of operations (AOs) designated by the JFC. Within their designated AOs, land and maritime force commanders integrate and synchronize maneuver, fires, and interdiction. To facilitate this integration and synchronization, such commanders have the authority to designate target priority, effects, and timing of fires within their AOs.

(1) Synchronization of efforts within land or maritime AOs with theater and/or joint operations area (JOA)-wide operations is of particular importance. To facilitate synchronization, the JFC establishes priorities that will be executed throughout the theater and/or JOA, including within the land and maritime force commander's AOs. The joint force air component commander (JFACC) is normally the supported commander for the JFC's overall air interdiction (AI) effort, while land and maritime component commanders are supported commanders for interdiction in their AOs.

(2) In coordination with the land and/or maritime force commander, those commanders designated by the JFC to execute theater and/or JOA-wide functions have the latitude to plan and execute these JFC prioritized operations within land and maritime AOs. Any commander executing such a mission within a land or maritime AO must coordinate the operation to avoid adverse effects and fratricide. If those operations would have adverse impact within a land or maritime AO, the commander assigned to execute the JOA-wide functions must readjust the plan, resolve the issue with the land or maritime component commander, or consult with the JFC for resolution.

(3) A joint special operations area (JSOA) is a restricted area of land, sea, and airspace, defined by a JFC who has geographic responsibilities, for use by a joint special operations component or joint special operations task force (JSOTF) for the conduct of special operations (SO) (e.g., a discrete direct action mission or longer term unconventional warfare operations). JFCs may use a JSOA to delineate and facilitate simultaneous conventional and SO. Within the JSOA, the joint force special operations component commander (JFSOCC) is the supported commander.

c. **Unity of Effort.** Component forces' planning, execution, and TA capabilities often overlap. Due to the diversity of systems capable of providing joint fire support, C2, and TA, the JFC must ensure unity of effort throughout the joint force.

4. Synchronization of Maneuver and Fires

a. Combining joint fire support and maneuver relies on the fundamental and beneficial effects of teamwork, unity of effort, and synchronization of capabilities in time, space, and purpose. As a principle of war, maneuver is the movement of forces in relation to the enemy to secure or retain positional advantage, usually in order to deliver — or threaten delivery of — the direct and indirect fires of the maneuvering force. Maneuver positions forces at decisive points to achieve surprise, psychological shock, physical momentum, and massed effects. The focus of maneuver is to render opponents incapable of resisting by shattering their morale and physical cohesion (their ability to fight as an effective, coordinated whole) rather than by destroying them physically through attrition.

See Joint Publication (JP) 3-0, Joint Operations, *for a more detailed discussion on maneuver.*

> *"Battles are won by fire and by movement. The purpose of the movement is to get the fire in a more advantageous place to play on the enemy. This is from the rear or flank."*
>
> **George S. Patton Jr.**
> ***War As I Knew It***

b. **Maneuver and joint fire support are complementary functions that are essential to achieving JFC objectives.** Maneuver is conducted to achieve positional advantage in respect to the enemy action to accomplish the mission. The principal purpose of maneuver is to gain positional advantage relative to the enemy COG in order to control or destroy associated critical capabilities (CCs). Maneuver of forces relative to enemy CCs can be key to the JFC's operation. Through maneuver, the JFC concentrates forces at decisive points to achieve surprise, psychological shock, and physical momentum. **Chances of successful maneuver are improved with fire support and movement.** Joint fire support destroys, neutralizes, or suppresses enemy forces and disrupts enemy maneuver, both on the surface and in the air, and influences populations which assists the maneuver of friendly forces. Joint fire support may be used separately from or in combination with maneuver to achieve strategic objectives or destroy, neutralize, or suppress enemy ground, maritime, and air forces, and influence populations. Through effective maneuver of friendly forces, the enemy can be placed into a position of disadvantage. If the enemy remains in position, their forces may be isolated and destroyed by fires delivered by land, air, maritime, and SOF. If the enemy withdraws, attempts to establish new defensive positions, or maneuvers their forces for counterattack, they may be exposed to unacceptable losses caused by the effective use of joint fire support. When exploiting the effects of maneuver, commanders use joint fire support to neutralize the enemy's forces and destroy their will to fight. Maneuver and firepower (joint fire support) are complementary dynamics of combat power. Although one might dominate a phase of the battle, their synchronization is a characteristic of successful military operations. The synchronization of fires and maneuver makes the defeat of larger enemy forces feasible and enhances the protection of friendly forces.

c. **Prevention of Fratricide.** The destructive power and range of modern weapons, coupled with the high intensity and rapid tempo of modern combat, increase the potential for fratricide. Risk management must become fully integrated while planning and executing operations. **Commanders must identify and assess situations that increase the risk of fratricide.** Commanders then incorporate guidance into all plans to minimize and control risks by implementing preventive measures. The primary preventive measures for limiting fratricide are comprehensive combat identification (CID) training, command emphasis, disciplined operations, control measures, fire support coordination measures (FSCMs), airspace coordinating measures (ACMs), close coordination among component commands, rehearsals, reliable and interoperable coordination systems, battle tracking, and enhanced situational awareness (SA). Recent developments in automation and blue force tracking tools, as well as any singular preventative measures identified above, assist in preventing fratricide, but must not be used as a sole means for clearance of fires. The risk of fratricide is greatly reduced when engagement decisions are vested with well-trained and qualified personnel. However, there is a trade-off between reducing fratricide with restrictive rules and enduring higher friendly casualties by the enemy. Therefore, fire support coordination and synchronization must be emphasized by the JFC. Special instructions may also specify particular means to prevent fratricide in specific missions.

d. **Effects.** Typically, the execution of joint fire support has an immediate or near term effect on the conduct of friendly operations. Component commanders employ joint fires to create the effects described in their CONOPS by synchronizing fires against the enemy. Detailed integration and coordination with supported and supporting forces is required. Planning allows detailed integration of joint fire support assets for anticipated time-sensitive targets (TSTs) and other immediate targets.

e. **Nonlethal Fires.** Nonlethal fires are any fires that do not directly seek the physical destruction of the intended target and are designed to impair, disrupt, or delay the performance of enemy forces, functions, or facilities, or to alter the behavior of an adversary. Nonlethal fires can be created using nonlethal or lethal weapons/capabilities. Nonlethal fires are primarily employed so as to incapacitate personnel or materiel, while minimizing fatalities, permanent injury to personnel, and undesired damage to property and the environment. Employment of nonlethal fires and other nonlethal capabilities must be integrated into operations to produce synergistic results. Examples include masking smoke, nighttime area illumination, area denial, and employment of some information operations (IO) capabilities, such as electronic attack (EA) and computer network attack (CNA), that deceive the enemy, disable the enemy's C2 systems, and disrupt operations. The employment of nonlethal fires is especially important when restraint and limitations on the use of deadly force are directed.

5. **Synchronizing and/or Integrating Maneuver and Interdiction**

Interdiction is an action to divert, disrupt, delay, or destroy the enemy's military surface capability before it can be used effectively against friendly forces, or to otherwise achieve objectives.

a. Synchronizing and/or integrating interdiction and maneuver (air, land, and maritime) provides one of the most dynamic concepts available to the joint force. Interdiction and maneuver usually are not considered separate operations against a common enemy, but rather normally are considered complementary operations designed to achieve the military strategic and operational objectives. Moreover, maneuver by air, land, or maritime forces can be conducted to interdict enemy military potential. Potential responses to integrated and synchronized maneuver and interdiction can create a dilemma for the enemy. If the enemy attempts to counter the maneuver, enemy forces may be exposed to unacceptable losses from interdiction. If the enemy employs measures to reduce such interdiction losses, enemy forces may not be able to counter the maneuver. The synergistic combined arms effect created by integrating and synchronizing interdiction and maneuver assists commanders in optimizing leverage at the operational level.

b. The land or maritime commander should clearly articulate the vision of maneuver operations to other commanders that may employ interdiction forces within the land or maritime AO. The land or maritime commander's intent and CONOPS should clearly state how interdiction will enable or enhance land or maritime force maneuver in the AO and what is to be accomplished with interdiction (as well as those actions to be avoided, such as the destruction of key transportation nodes or the use of certain munitions in a specific area). Once this is understood, other interdiction-capable commanders normally can plan and execute their operations with only that coordination required with the land or maritime commander. However, the land or maritime commander should provide other interdiction-capable commanders as much latitude as possible in the planning and execution of interdiction operations within the AO.

c. JFCs must prioritize activities to support the maneuver and interdiction needs of all forces and take action to mitigate any factor interfering with their effective employment. In addition to normal target nomination procedures, JFCs establish procedures through which land or maritime force commanders can specifically identify those interdiction targets they are unable to engage with organic assets within their operational areas that could affect planned or ongoing maneuver. These targets may be identified individually or by category, specified geographically, or tied to a desired effect or time period. Interdiction target priorities within the land or maritime AOs are considered along with theater and/or JOA-wide interdiction priorities by JFCs and are reflected in all the related resourcing decisions. The JFACC uses these priorities to plan, coordinate, and execute the theater and/or JOA-wide AI effort. The purpose of these procedures is to afford added visibility to, and allow JFCs to give priority to, targets directly affecting planned maneuver by air, land, or maritime forces.

See JP 3-03, Joint Interdiction, *for a more detailed discussion of interdiction.*

CHAPTER II
JOINT FIRE SUPPORT COMMAND AND CONTROL

> *"A superiority of fire, and therefore a superiority in directing and delivering fire and in making use of fire, will become the main factors upon which the efficiency of a force will depend."*
>
> **Marshal of France Ferdinand Foch**
> *Precepts and Judgments, 1919*

1. Introduction

This chapter reviews the joint force command structure and the fire support functions employed to control joint fires. It includes their roles, responsibilities, and some of the targeting systems available to them. The successful application of joint fire support depends on the close coordination of these functions. Joint fire support must function in a coordinated and integrated manner to support the commander's objectives.

2. Joint Fire Support Command and Control

a. Joint Force Commander and Staff

(1) **Joint Force Commander.** The JFC, using systems that allow rapid response to changes as they occur, is responsible for ensuring the synchronization and integration of joint fires. The challenge for the JFC is to integrate and synchronize the wide range of capabilities at his disposal. The JFC's intent will normally be to bring force against the opponent's entire structure in a near simultaneous manner to overwhelm and cripple the enemy's capabilities and will to resist. In this effort, liaison elements play a pivotal role in the coordination of joint fire support.

(2) **Directorate of Operations**

(a) The operations directorate of a joint staff (J-3) serves as the JFC's principal staff advisor for the coordination, integration, and synchronization of joint fire support with other major elements of operations such as C2, intelligence, movement and maneuver, protection, and sustainment. These functions may include:

<u>1.</u> Developing estimates of the situation and courses of action (COAs).

<u>2.</u> Developing mission-type orders and guidance for JFC approval.

<u>3.</u> Developing operation orders (OPORDs), and operation plans (OPLANs).

<u>4.</u> Developing joint fire support targeting guidance, objectives, and priorities for JFC approval.

5. Coordinating and assessing joint operations.

6. Coordinating ROE.

7. Recommending, coordinating, reviewing, designating, and disseminating FSCMs, maneuver control measures, ACMs as part of overall concept of the operations for joint fires and joint fire support.

8. Maintaining munitions supply status and logistic concerns affecting joint force operations.

9. Ensuring IO are fully integrated and synchronized with operations.

10. Establishing a joint fires element (JFE).

11. Organizing and serving as a member of a joint targeting coordination board (JTCB), if established by the JFC.

(b) The JFC may approve the formation of a JFE within the J-3. The JFE is an optional staff element comprised of representatives from the J-3, the components, and other elements of the JFC's staff, to include the intelligence directorate of a joint staff targeting staff, logistics directorate of a joint staff, plans directorate of a joint staff, and others as required. (See Figure II-1.) The JFE is an integrating staff element that synchronizes and coordinates fires planning and coordination on behalf of the JFC and should be physically located near the joint task force (JTF) joint operations center, collocated with the IO cell if possible. The JFE assists the J-3 in accomplishing responsibilities and tasks as a staff advisor to the JFC. JFE key functions and tasks generally include the following:

1. Develops JOA-wide joint targeting guidance, objectives, and priorities (normally accomplished in conjunction with component planners as part of the joint planning group [JPG]).

2. Coordinates, deconflicts, and validates target nominations at the JFC level and higher.

3. Coordinates component input to the joint integrated prioritized target list (JIPTL). Prioritizes and forwards the JIPTL to the JTCB for review and approval and then manages the approved JIPTL.

4. Coordinates, maintains, and disseminates a complete list of FSCMs within the JOA to avoid fratricide and deconflicts with other current or future operations, to include managing the restricted target list (RTL) and NSL.

5. Develops the roles, functions, and agenda of the JTCB for JFC approval.

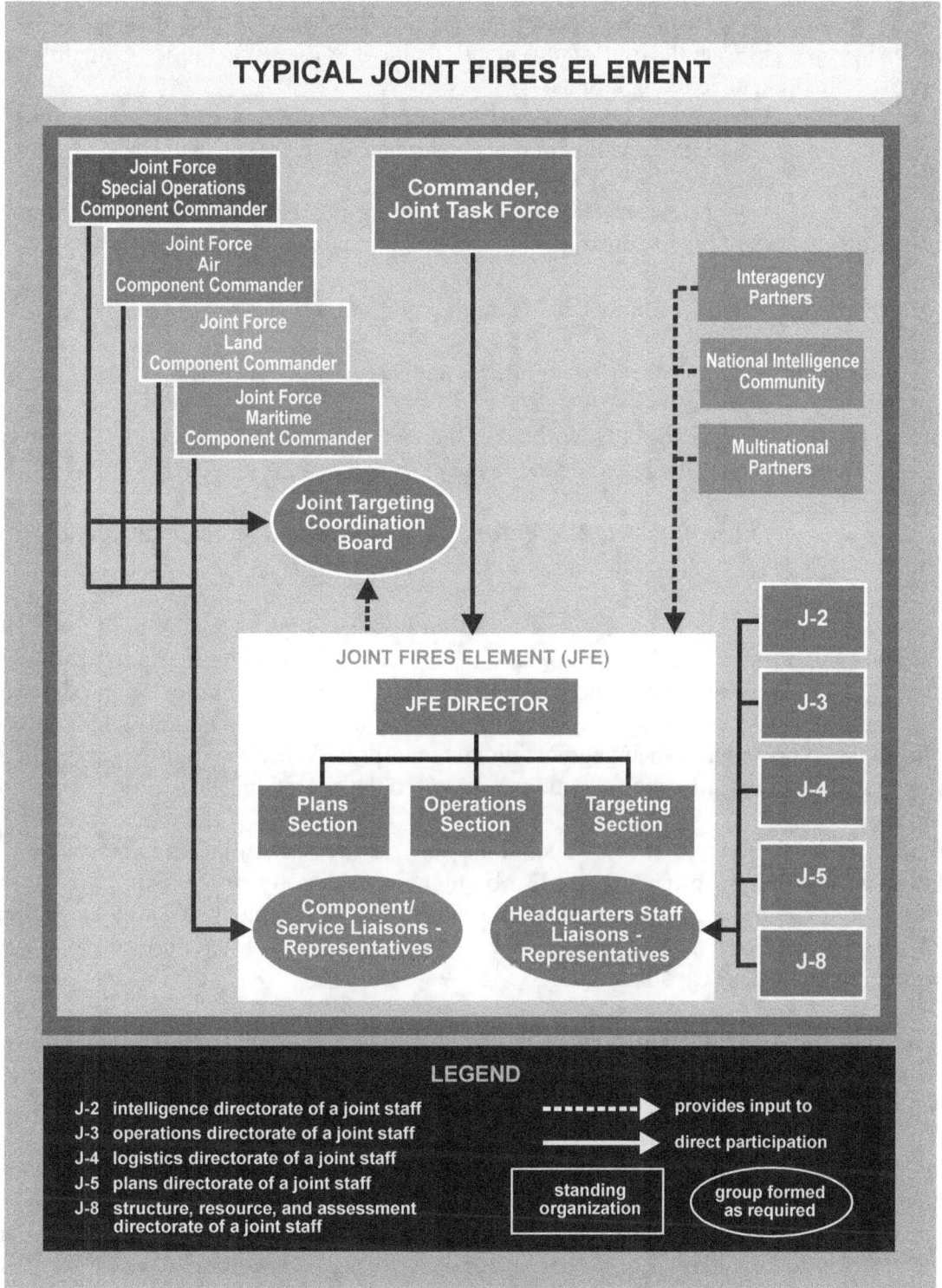

Figure II-1. Typical Joint Fires Element

    <u>6.</u> Organizes a strategy team to address intermediate targeting efforts to bridge the gap between current and future operations.

7. Reviews/recommends intelligence, surveillance, and reconnaissance (ISR) collection requirements to include assisting the joint intelligence support element in developing targets.

8. Develops the joint fires estimate and COAs.

9. Monitors TST and component-critical target operations for the J-3. Recommends procedures for engaging TSTs and component-critical targets.

10. Recommends JTF high-payoff targets (HPTs) to the JPG.

11. Coordinates joint fires and targeting ROE issues.

12. Develops collateral damage prevention procedures based on commanders' guidance and higher level directives.

13. Conducts assessments of joint fires and targeting in coordination with higher HQ and components.

(c) J-3 staffing may vary based on how the JFC forms the joint force HQ and the component forces for the operation. The J-3's augmentation requirements will depend on a variety of factors, including the mission, expected complexity and duration of the operation, peacetime staffing levels, expertise of the new operations staff, and the joint force composition. Such augmentation should provide the capability to accomplish fires planning and coordination functions relevant to the operation.

(d) Some joint force operations may require only limited augmentation. In this case, the JFC might choose to absorb augmentees directly into existing joint force staff sections and divisions. For example, the JFC may augment the joint operations center with additional personnel from the combatant commands or Services to ensure continuous operations capability.

(e) Information systems bring critical information together for collation, collaboration, interpretation, and analysis to enable decisionmaking. Information systems, personnel, equipment, and a variety of related procedures support the execution of joint fire support missions. Unity of effort is key to the effective coordination of joint fire support. Vertical and horizontal integration is also essential for effective joint fire support. For this reason, Service and functional components provide a hierarchy of coordinators, coordination agencies, and liaison officers that interface with commanders at each level of execution. These coordinators have one goal in common — to effectively direct the integration and employment of joint fire support to accomplish the mission.

(3) **Joint Force Staff Functions.** To effectively plan joint fire support, planners must understand the objective, purpose of the operation, and the commander's intent. Subordinate JFCs will translate the combatant commander's guidance and strategy into clearly defined and attainable operational level objectives. They then write

supporting OPLANs and OPORDs to attain those objectives. These plans and orders will contain a CONOPS that describes joint force employment. Joint fire support priorities and goals are typically listed as part of the overall priorities and goals within the CONOPS. The commander's estimate and the CONOPS assist in focusing the employment of all assets, to include those providing joint fire support.

(a) **Commander and Staff Estimates.** Estimates help the commander clearly understand the situation and select the best COA. The estimate results in an accurate visualization of the current enemy and friendly situation, a visualization of the goal or mission, and a clear expression of COAs. Consideration of how to employ fires continues throughout the estimate process.

(b) **Concept of Operations.** The CONOPS is key in describing how the commander anticipates the operation unfolding. The concept is based on the commander's selected COA and describes where and how friendly forces engage the enemy. In the CONOPS, the commander describes how the action of each of the components or supporting commands fit together to accomplish the assigned mission. The CONOPS discusses joint force maneuver and the application of joint fire support. The joint fires discussion should reflect the JFC's concept for application of available fires assets. Guidance for joint fire support should address the following:

1. Joint force policies, procedures, and planning cycles.

2. Joint fire support assets for planning purposes.

3. Priorities for employing TA assets.

4. Areas that require joint fire support to support operational maneuver.

5. TSTs.

6. High-value targets (HVTs) and HPTs.

7. Anticipated joint fire support requirements.

8. FSCMs.

(4) **Synchronizing Command and Control Assets.** The JFC utilizes C2 to synchronize efforts in a number of key areas, such as ISR. Appropriate joint, Service, and national agencies engaged in ISR activities must support the efforts to integrate and synchronize fires. To support the synchronization of fires, C2 must be responsive to the user, and be capable of real-time information management and data processing.

See JP 2-0, Joint Intelligence, *and JP 6-0,* Joint Communications System.

b. **Joint Targeting Coordination Board.** The JFC has the responsibility to conduct planning, coordination, and deconfliction associated with joint targeting. Typically, the JFC establishes a JTCB and appoints the deputy JFC or a component commander to chair it. When a JTCB is not established and the JFC decides not to delegate targeting oversight, the JFC may perform this task at the joint force HQ. If the JFC so designates, a JTCB may be either an integrating center for this effort or a JFC-level review mechanism. In either case, it should be comprised of representatives from the staff, all components and, if required, their subordinate units. The primary focus of the JTCB is to ensure target priorities, guidance, and the associated effects are linked to the JFC's objectives. Briefings conducted at the JTCB should focus on ensuring that targeting efforts are coordinated and synchronized with intelligence and operations (by all components and applicable staff elements). The JTCB must also maintain a current joint target list, RTL, NSL, and current and planned FSCMs. (The JFC JFE will receive component lists and FSCMs, then collate and disseminate current and planned target lists and FSCMs.) The JTCB may assist the JFC in developing or revising the targeting guidance and/or priorities. The JTCB maintains a macro-level view of the operational area and ensures targeting nominations are consistent with the JFC's intent. In a multinational environment, the JTCB may be subordinate to a multinational targeting coordination board.

See JP 3-60, Joint Targeting.

c. **Combined Enterprise Regional Information Exchange System (CENTRIXS)**

(1) When conducting multinational operations, some contributing nations may not have connectivity to the joint force information systems. This will require an additional communications system to ensure that these forces and organizations have interoperability to remain a viable contribution to the multinational effort.

(2) The JFC can facilitate information sharing by coordinating with the supported commanders to establish a coalition local area network such as the CENTRIXS. **CENTRIXS provides one example of establishing and maintaining multinational connectivity at the tactical and operational level, with reachback capability to the strategic level.**

d. **Component Fires Command and Control**

(1) **Joint Force Land Component**

(a) **US Army Joint Fire Support Command and Control Agencies.** Fire support personnel are assigned at all levels from company to theater army (which may also be the Army Service component commander or joint force land component commander [JFLCC] HQ). A company fire support officer (FSO) leads the fire support team (FIST). Battalion/squadron/brigade combat team FSOs lead the fires cell at their respective HQ and are assisted by subordinate FSOs and fire support noncommissioned officers (NCOs). The commander of the brigade combat team's fires battalion is identified as the fire support coordinator and the commander's primary advisor on the planning for and employment of field artillery (FA) and fire support and the integrations of lethal and nonlethal fires. The chief of fires (COF) leads the fires cell found from division to theater army level. He is assisted by cell FSOs and fire support NCOs. The fires cell can send representatives (FSOs and/or fire support NCOs) fires elements to other sections or cells within the HQ. These fire support personnel advise the commander on fire support capabilities and joint fire support C2, effective use of fires assets, and assist in the planning, coordination, and execution of fires.

1. **Chief of Fires (Army).** The US Army COF is the senior FA officer permanently assigned as the full-time fire support staff advisor to the commander and staff at division and higher HQ. The COF performs all the staff functions associated with fire support. Additionally, as fire support cell supervisor, the COF works with the commander and his staff to integrate fire support and IO (core supporting and related capabilities) with each other and into the unit's concept of operation.

2. **Battlefield Coordination Detachment (BCD).** The US Army provides a BCD as the interface for selected operational environment functions between the Army forces (ARFOR) and the air commander, or the US Air Force Service component commander. A BCD is collocated with the joint air operations center (JAOC), combined air operations center, or the Air Force air and space operations center (AOC). The BCD interface includes exchanging current intelligence and operational data, support requirements, coordinating the integration of ARFOR requirements for ACMs, FSCMs, and theater airlift. A BCD can also be tasked to perform ARFOR interface duties for subordinate US Army HQ. The BCD is not a fire support cell, but acts as the ARFOR senior liaison element and also can perform many fires functions. When a US Army HQ is the land commander, the BCD serves as the land commander's liaison to the air component commander.

3. **Liaison.** Although liaison elements from other Services are found at supported Army units, various liaison elements such as Marine liaison, naval air liaison, special operations liaison element (SOLE), and Navy surface operations liaison elements usually link up with the BCD at the JAOC when appropriate. Typically, ground liaison officers for fighter and airlift wings and other liaison officers may also be provided.

4. **Fires Cell.** The fires cell of the theater army operational command post oversees the application of joint fire support, artillery, rockets, and offensive IO in support of theater army operations. Responsibilities include:

a. Coordinating and synchronizing all aspects of operational fires with component commands, major subordinate commands, and multinational forces.

b. Synchronizing fires with other governmental agencies.

<u>c.</u> Overseeing the development of the theater army operational fires objectives, supporting target nominations, and attack guidance through the execution of joint boards and cells.

<u>d.</u> Participating as members of the joint and theater army target coordination board, candidate target review boards, and other boards as required.

See Field Manual (FM) 3-09, Fire Support.

<u>5.</u> **US Army Air and Missile Defense Command (AAMDC).** The AAMDC is the Army's operational lead for theater air and missile defense (TAMD) and plans, coordinates, integrates, and synchronizes the operational elements of TAMD. The AAMDC, normally collocated with the JAOC, operates in direct support (DS) of the area air defense commander (AADC) and is fully integrated into the AADC's air defense C2 system. The AAMDC attack operations cell and intelligence section integrated within the JAOC conduct analysis and targeting focused specifically against the theater missile (TM) threat. Analysis includes such actions as developing TM information requirements, building operational patterns and profiles, identifying trigger events, analyzing launch events, conducting countermobility analysis, and identifying electronic warfare (EW) vulnerabilities. TM targeting actions include nominating attack strategies and submitting target nominations and mission requests directly to the JAOC. When appropriate, the AAMDC commander or representative participates in the JTCB. Also, the AAMDC and BCD will coordinate and synchronize their operations at the JAOC.

See FM 3-01.20/Air Force Tactics, Techniques, and Procedures (Instruction) (AFTTP[I]) 3-2.30, Multi-Service Tactics, Techniques, and Procedures for JAOC/AAMDC Coordination.

(b) **US Marine Corps Joint Fires Command and Control Agencies.** Depending upon the mission, the decision of the JFC, and their capabilities, US Marine Corps (USMC) forces may be employed as the joint force land component, as part of the joint force land component, as the joint force maritime component or as part of the joint force maritime component, or as the joint force air component. Marine Corps forces will operate as a Marine air-ground task force (MAGTF) consisting of a command element, a ground combat element (GCE), an aviation combat element (ACE), and a logistics combat element. The MAGTF commander will retain operational control (OPCON) of organic air assets. The primary mission of the MAGTF ACE is the support of the MAGTF GCE. During joint operations, the MAGTF air assets normally will be in support of the MAGTF mission. The MAGTF commander will make sorties available to the JFC, for tasking through the JFACC, for air defense, long-range interdiction, and long-range reconnaissance. Sorties in excess of MAGTF DS requirements will be provided to the JFC for tasking through the JFACC for the support of other components of the joint force or the joint force as a whole. Various agencies and elements exist within the MAGTFs to assist commanders in the execution of their fires responsibilities. These agencies may be used for either landing force (LF) or sustained land operations. The Marine expeditionary force (MEF) command element organizes a force fires coordination center (FFCC), which is responsible for overall fires coordination. At each level below the MEF command element (division, regiment, and battalion), a fire support coordination center (FSCC) is established as an advisory and coordination agency within the GCE. The FFCC and each FSCC is staffed with representatives of the various Marine Corps and Navy supporting arms whose roles differ at the various levels. For example, during the initial phase of an amphibious operation, while control and coordination responsibility of supporting arms is still afloat, the MAGTF typically provides the LF representation in the Navy's supporting arms coordination center (SACC).

See JP 1, Doctrine for the Armed Forces of the United States, *for additional information.*

<u>1</u>. **Commanders.** In an amphibious operation, the commander, amphibious task force (CATF), exercises the overall responsibility for coordination of naval surface fire support (NSFS), air support, and LF artillery fire support. When the commander, landing force (CLF), normally the MAGTF commander, is established ashore, the CATF may pass this responsibility to the CLF. Once the passage of control ashore is executed, the CLF will coordinate fires within the AO. When control is afloat, the senior naval fire support coordination agency is the SACC.

See JP 3-02, Joint Doctrine for Amphibious Operations.

<u>2</u>. **Liaison.** LF representatives coordinate requests of LF elements ashore, monitor fire support activities, and plan additional requirements. This includes continued liaison with the SACC and close coordination with the Marine air command and control system (MACCS). LF representatives in the SACC make appropriate recommendations regarding troop safety, type and means of delivery, and record all target information for future reference ashore. Once control passes ashore, the MAGTF commander executes responsibilities through the FFCC or FSCC ashore. This responsibility includes continued liaison with the SACC along with close coordination with the MACCS.

<u>3</u>. **Force Fires Coordination Center.** The FFCC is the senior fire support organization for the MAGTF. As such, it assists the MAGTF commander in the planning, coordination, execution, and assessment of fires for a MAGTF. While the FFCC assists the commander in fighting the single battle, its focus is on the deep fight. The FFCC coordinates those matters that cannot be coordinated by the GCE (FSCC), ACE Marine tactical air command center (TACC), or combat service support operations center for integration of fire support plans. Additionally, it assists in providing fires in support of close and rear fight. FFCC liaisons are sourced to provide close and continuous coordination.

<u>4</u>. **Fire Support Coordination Center.** The FSCC is a single location that centralizes communications facilities and personnel for the coordination of all forms of fire support for the GCE. The USMC employs a designated ground combat officer as a fire support coordinator (FSC), who acts as the direct representative of the CLF for the planning and coordinating of all available fire support. The FSCC is organized and

supervised by the FSC and is collocated with, and in support of, the operations officer. A USMC FSCC normally includes an air section, naval gunfire liaison section, and artillery section to plan and execute fires in support of the scheme of maneuver. Additionally, a mortar section may be included in the FSCC for an infantry battalion, but will not be found at any other level of C2 for fire support coordination.

5. **Tactical Air Command Center.** The Marine TACC is the senior agency of the MACCS. It provides the facilities for the commander of the ACE and the battlestaff to command, supervise, and direct MAGTF air operations. The Marine TACC is usually established ashore incrementally, beginning with a tactical air direction center (TADC). When the commander of Marine Corps forces is also the JFACC, he will augment the Marine Corps TACC with elements from other components to create a JAOC.

6. **Direct Air Support Center (DASC).** The DASC is an organization within the MACCS and serves as the Marine Corps central coordination point for all aircraft support to GCE-user agencies at all echelons. The DASC assigns direct air support aircraft to terminal control agencies, provides aircraft ingress and egress route instructions, and disseminates advisory information. When control is afloat, the Navy tactical air control center (TACC) supervises the ashore DASC's operation. When control is ashore, the Marine TADC or Marine TACC supervises the DASC's operations. The DASC is normally the first major air control agency to land in an amphibious operation. The DASC becomes operational when control of the operation is passed ashore and collocates (physically or electronically) with the senior FSCC.

7. **Marine Corps Tactical Air Control Party (TACP).** The Marine Corps TACP establishes and maintains facilities for liaison and communications between supported units and appropriate control agencies. An air officer leads the TACP, normally with three teams assigned per maneuver battalion. Their mission is to inform and advise the supported ground unit commander on the employment of supporting aircraft and to request and coordinate air support missions. In addition, the TACP provides terminal attack control for close air support (CAS) missions.

8. **Tactical Air Operations Center (TAOC).** The Marine Corps TAOC is subordinate to the Marine Corps TACC. Among its duties, the TAOC provides safe passage, radar control, and surveillance for CAS aircraft en route to and from target areas.

9. **Shore Fire Control Party (SFCP).** The supporting Marine Corps artillery battalions provide SFCPs to supported units. The SFCP consists of an NSFS liaison team and an NSFS spotting team. The NSFS liaison team is specifically organized to handle NSFS liaison matters for the supported commander, while the spotting team is charged with requesting and adjusting fires of assigned DS ships and general support (GS) ships.

(2) **Joint Force Maritime Component/Commander Navy Forces**

(a) **Supporting Arms Coordination Center.** The SACC is configured with the communications facilities required to coordinate artillery, air, and naval surface fires. Functioning as a fire support coordinating element for the maritime forces, the SACC is supervised by the supporting arms coordinator. During amphibious operations, the SACC is the primary agency that coordinates and controls all supporting fires for the CATF to establish the LF ashore.

(b) **Navy Tactical Air Control System.** The Navy tactical air control system is the principal air control system afloat. The senior Navy air control agency is the Navy TACC. During amphibious operations, and before control is passed ashore, Navy TACC controls all air operations within the amphibious objective area (AOA). The Navy TACC is responsible for planning and conducting air operations, including CAS. Typically, the Navy TACC is onboard the amphibious task force (ATF) flagship. If the JFACC's command operations center is afloat, the Navy TACC may support operations for the JAOC. The Navy TACC has two sections that control and integrate CAS:

<u>1</u>. **Air Traffic Control Section (ATCS).** The ATCS provides initial safe passage, radar control, and surveillance for CAS aircraft in the AOA. The ATCS can also provide early detection, identification, and warning of enemy aircraft.

<u>2</u>. **Air Support Control Section.** The air support control section supports the Navy TACC by controlling, supporting, or transferring control to subsidiary tactical air direction controllers afloat or ashore. The section is located in the SACC and coordinates with the Navy TACC to assist in the deconfliction of air missions, routes, and requests for fires.

(3) **Joint Force Air Component Commander.** JFCs normally will designate a JFACC, whose authority and responsibilities are defined by the establishing JFC based on the JFC's CONOPS. See JP 3-0, *Joint Operations*, and JP 1, *Doctrine for the Armed Forces of the United States*, for additional guidance on the organization of joint forces. Conversely, a transition from JFACC to JFC staff may also be directed when the JFC determines that operational requirements warrant such a change. The Air Force, Navy, or Marine Corps component commander may be designated as the JFACC. However, the following discussion is based upon US Air Force fires C2 capabilities when the commander Air Force forces is designated as the JFACC. The JFACC normally exercises OPCON over US Air Force forces through the theater air ground system and exercises tactical control or has a support relationship with other forces/capabilities made available for tasking. The focal point for tasking and exercising control of these forces is the JAOC. The JAOC performs the tasks of planning, coordinating, controlling, reporting, and monitoring the execution of joint air operations.

(a) **Joint Air Operations Center.** The JAOC is structured to operate as a fully integrated node and staffed by members of all participating components to fulfill the air commander's responsibilities. The JAOC synchronizes air operations with joint force air, land, and sea operations through centralized planning, direction, and coordination of air operations. The JAOC is the senior joint air power C2 element in the joint force and is the JFACC's agent for providing centralized planning and decentralized execution of joint air operations. The JAOC typically produces the joint air operations plan, air tasking order (ATO), airspace control plan, and air defense plan.

See JP 3-30, Command and Control for Joint Air Operations, *for additional detailed guidance on JAOC operations.*

(b) **Air Support Operations Center (ASOC).** The ASOC is the principal Air Force C2 node for integrating air power into Army land operations. As a direct subordinate element of the JAOC, the ASOC is responsible for the direction and control of air operations directly supporting the Army land operation. It processes and coordinates air missions requiring integration with other supporting arms and ground forces. The ASOC is usually collocated with the senior Army tactical echelon, and coordinates operations with the permanently aligned TACP and the JAOC. The ASOC has five primary functions. It manages CAS assets within the supported ground commander's AO; processes CAS requests and controls the flow of CAS aircraft; deconflicts airspace coordination measures and fire support coordinating measures with aircraft; assigns and directs attack aircraft, when authorized, to the joint terminal attack controllers (JTACs); and manages the Air Force air request net and its specific tactical air direction net frequencies. Additionally, the ASOC may also coordinate in other mission areas, to include AI, air defense, ISR, joint suppression of enemy air defenses (J-SEAD), and joint personnel recovery.

(c) **Tactical Air Control Party.** The TACP is the principal Air Force liaison element collocated with Army maneuver units from battalion through corps. The TACP has two primary missions: advise ground commanders on the capabilities and limitations of air operations, and provide the primary terminal attack control of CAS. TACPs coordinate ACMs and deconflict aircraft with Army fire support. TACPs are organized into expeditionary air support operations groups or squadrons that are aligned with their respective Army corps, division, or brigade HQ.

(d) **Forward Air Controller (Airborne) (FAC[A]).** The FAC(A) is a specifically trained and qualified aviation officer who exercises control from the air of aircraft engaged in CAS of ground troops. The FAC(A) is normally an airborne extension of the TACP. The FAC(A) also provides coordination and terminal attack control for CAS missions as well as locating, marking, and attacking ground targets using other fire support assets.

(e) **Tactical Air Coordinator (Airborne) (TAC[A]).** The TAC(A) is an officer who coordinates, from an aircraft, the actions of other aircraft engaged in air support of ground or sea forces. The TAC(A) also expedites CAS aircraft-to-JTAC handoff during "heavy traffic" CAS operations.

(f) **Joint Fires Observer (JFO).** A JFO is a trained and certified Service member who can request, adjust, and control surface-to-surface fires, provide targeting information in support of Type 2 and Type 3 CAS terminal attack control, and perform autonomous terminal guidance operations (TGO). JFOs provide the capability to exploit those opportunities that exist in the operational environment where a trained observer could be used to efficiently support air delivered fires, surface-to-surface fires, and facilitate targeting. JFOs cannot perform terminal attack control of CAS missions and do not replace a trained and certified JTAC.

(g) **Joint Terminal Attack Controller.** A JTAC is a qualified (certified) Service member who, from a forward position, directs the action of combat aircraft engaged in CAS and other offensive air operations. A qualified and current JTAC will be recognized across the Department of Defense (DOD) as capable and authorized to perform all types of terminal attack control.

See JP 3-09.3, Close Air Support, *for more detailed information about C2 of CAS operations*.

(h) **The Control and Reporting Center (CRC).** The CRC is a deployable battle management platform employed at the tactical level to support joint air operations. It is directly subordinate to the Air Force AOC and can operate independently or in combination with other C2 elements. CRC operators are able to support all the same mission areas as Airborne Warning and Control System (AWACS) although limited by line of sight communications and radar coverage. The JAOC assigns the CRC a geographic area, within which it manages all air defense, offensive air and airspace management activities. The CRC can disseminate air defense warnings and an air picture to other C2 nodes through data links and its extensive communications capabilities.

(i) **Joint Air Component Coordination Element (JACCE).** The JFACC may establish one or more JACCEs with other commanders' HQ to better integrate joint air operations with their operations. When established, the JACCE is a component level liaison that serves as the direct representative of the JFACC. A JACCE is normally made up of the liaison element(s) of the Service designated to provide the JFACC. The JACCE does not perform any C2 functions and the JACCE director does not have command authority over any air forces. The JACCE facilitates the integration of joint air power by exchanging current intelligence, operational data, support requirements, and by coordinating the integration of JFACC requirements for ACMs, FSCMs, personnel recovery, and CAS. JACCE expertise should include plans, operations, ISR, space, airspace management, air mobility, and administrative and communications support.

(4) **Special Operations Component**

(a) The JFSOCC exercises overall responsibility for coordination of all fire support in support of SO and, when tasked, fire support using SOF assets in support of other elements of the joint force. SOF coordinate fire support through both external and SOF channels. Within SOF channels, various elements are established to assist commanders in the execution of their fire support responsibilities. SOF elements that provide C2 and/or liaison capabilities include:

1. **Joint Special Operations Task Force.** The JSOTF is a JTF composed of SO units from more than one Service, formed to carry out a specific special operation or prosecute SO in support of a theater campaign or other operations. The JSOTF may have conventional units assigned or attached to support the conduct of specific missions. The JSOTF staff coordinates joint fire support with other components of the joint force and US Government agencies. As appropriate, the staff can form a JFE.

2. **Joint Special Operations Air Component Commander (JSOACC).** The JSOACC is the commander within a joint SO command responsible for planning and executing joint SO air activities, and for ensuring effective coordination, synchronization, and integration of such activities with conventional air operations. The JSOACC will normally be the commander with the preponderance of aviation assets and/or greatest ability to plan, coordinate, allocate, task, control, and support assigned and attached SO aviation assets. When a joint special operations air component is established as a functional component of a JSOTF, the commander, joint special operations task force (CDRJSOTF) normally exercises OPCON of all assigned and attached joint SO aviation assets through the JSOACC. However, there are also circumstances where the CDRJSOTF may elect to place selected SO aviation assets under separate control. A key responsibility of the JSOACC is to ensure close liaison is accomplished with other SOF components and with the conventional air components of other Service and/or functional component commands. The JSOACC ensures liaison with the JFACC is accomplished through the SOLE in the JFACC's JAOC. Through the SOLE, the JSOACC ensures SO aviation activities are closely coordinated, synchronized, and integrated with the JFACC's operations to ensure airspace coordination, flight safety, operations security, and unity of effort.

3. **Naval Special Warfare Task Group (NSWTG) and Naval Special Warfare Task Unit (NSWTU).** Naval SOF assigned to the SO commander are normally under the C2 of an NSWTG or NSWTU. The NSWTG is a naval special warfare organization that plans, conducts, and supports SO in support of fleet commanders and SO commanders. The NSWTU is a subordinate unit of an NSWTG.

4. **Special Operations Command and Control Element (SOCCE).** The SOCCE is the focal point for the synchronization of SOF activities with land and maritime operations. The SOCCE is normally employed when SOF conduct operations in conjunction with a conventional force. It collocates with the command element of the supported commander and performs C2 or liaison functions directed by the SO commander. The focus of the coordination is on the synchronization of firepower and deconfliction of joint fires.

(b) **Special Operations Fire Support Coordination.** Liaison between SOF and other elements of the joint force is critical to both effective support and the prevention of fratricide. SOF liaison elements provide SOF expertise to coordinate, synchronize, and deconflict SO both in support of conventional forces and when SO are conducted unilaterally. SOF C2 organizations such as an NSWTG and/or NSWTU or SOCCE may provide (or act as) liaison elements for coordination of fire support with their respective Service components. Additionally, the following elements are capable of providing fire support coordination for SOF:

<u>1</u>. **Special Operations Liaison Element.** The SOLE is a team provided by the SO commander to the JFACC (if designated) or appropriate Service component air C2 organization to coordinate, deconflict, and integrate SO air, surface, and subsurface operations with conventional air operations. The SOLE director works directly for the SO commander and is not in the SOF chain of command, thus command authority for mission tasking, planning, and execution of SO remains with the SO commander. The SOLE director places SOF ground, maritime, and air liaison personnel in divisions of the JAOC to integrate with the SO staff. The SOLE coordinates appropriate FSCMs to help avoid fratricide.

<u>2</u>. **Special Tactics Team (STT).** STTs are a task-organized element of US Air Force SOF that may include combat control, pararescue, and SO weather personnel. Functions include austere airfield and assault zone reconnaissance, surveillance, establishment, and terminal control; tactical weather observations and forecasting; combat search and rescue; combat casualty care and evacuation staging; as well as coordinating, planning, and conducting air and ground fire support and terminal attack control. STTs are a part of the theater SOF and are normally under OPCON of the SO commander. When supporting air operations, tactical control of these teams should be assigned to the air commander through the AOC as an extension of the theater air control system. However, because the STT can be employed by both SOF and theater air structures, it is imperative that apportionment, allocation, command relationships, and control authority be clearly stated and understood by SO and air commanders.

<u>3</u>. **Special Operations Coordination Element (SOCOORD).** The SOCOORD serves as the primary advisor to a US Army corps or MEF commander with regard to SOF integration, capabilities, and limitations. The SOCOORD is a functional staff element of the corps (or MEF) operations officer and serves as the J-3 SOF advisor, with augmentation, if the corps (or MEF) is established as a JTF.

<u>4</u>. **Joint Air Component Coordination Element to the Special Operations Task Force.** The JFACC provides a JACCE to other commanders in the JOA to assist in coordinating joint air operations. For SOF, the JACCE will typically be located at the JSOTF and work with the JFE. The JACCE provides the JSOTF with air power expertise for both SOF and conventional air force assets. The JACCE represents the JFACC for joint air operations and the JSOACC commander at the JSOTF on issues relating to SOF and conventional air force integration into the ground scheme of maneuver. The JACCE is the focal point for all preplanned air requests (e.g., CAS, airlift, ISR, EW), and is responsible for validating JTAC's currency and qualifications upon entry into theater and tracking JTACs for all SOF components. The JACCE will be active in both future planning and current operations at the JSOTF, and will work closely

with the JFE to pass the most responsive assets to immediate engagements that may require fire support.

        5. **Joint Fires Element.** The SOF JFE plans, coordinates, synchronizes, and executes fire support to safeguard both friendly ground and air units while expediting joint fires. Together with the JACCE, the JFE will monitor and rapidly respond to SOF joint fires requests. The JFE/JACCE team can efficiently determine the most responsive resource and delivery means to respond to immediate support requests. The JFE consolidates FSCMs for the JSOTF, tracks team locations, and reports them to the SOLE to aid the air-ground deconfliction process.

    e. **Joint Fire Support Coordination, Targeting, Surveillance, and Management Systems**

      (1) **Joint Automated Deep Operations Coordination System (JADOCS)**

        (a) JADOCS facilitates the integration of joint/coalition fires. Digital integration of US and allied joint fires systems enables timely execution of TSTs, HPTs, and HVTs. The enhanced JADOCS allows for improved internal and external coordination/execution of immediate targets by providing a suite of tools and interfaces for horizontal and vertical integration across functional areas. It is currently installed on over 900 systems worldwide, is the baseline for the Naval Fires Control System, and is a major segment of the intelligence application package for theater battle management core system (TBMCS) functionality at wing and squadron levels. The automated four dimensional deconfliction capability aids in the reduction of fratricide, thereby expediting prosecution of targets,

        (b) The joint management function provides the ability to rapidly change and display operational graphics and FSCMs while conducting joint fire support. It uses the JADOCS engagement zone manager (EZM) and the common geographic reference system to portray operational and some tactical operational graphics and FSCMs for both linear and nonlinear situations. The EZM enables operators to quickly create and change FSCMs and coordinate them between components for rapid approval and display. When used in conjunction with the control measures manager, which enables rapid change and display of FSCMs, these tools enable the JFC and components to visualize friendly fires in three dimensions over any area. Operational graphics can also be overlaid with imagery and terrain data to improve SA and planning.

        (c) The AI planning and execution function provides more effective employment of AI assets through timely and improved information flow for the identification, assignment, and nomination of AI targets. It enables the joint force component commanders and staff to allocate air resources in a more efficient manner through early assessment of potential and planned missions. AI provides the ability to monitor ATO execution through all phases and provides immediate visibility into AI nominations throughout the targeting process, including periodic updates to tune AI missions and maximize joint fires.

(d) The counterfire-common operational picture (CF-COP) function provides a near real-time picture of the artillery battle. It allocates cannon and rocket resources for more efficient counterfire operations through digital integration at multi-echelons; from joint/multinational level down to tactical firing units. CF-COP also includes munitions allocation and status.

(e) The FSCMs analysis function provides a means for assessing changes and movements of the fire support coordination line (FSCL) on current and planned missions in the ATO. It provides immediate visibility of targets exposed or covered by movements in the FSCL and offers the JFC and staff opportunities to assess the consequences prior to movement.

(f) The multinational coordination and integration function facilitates the integration of coalition artillery with respect to both the counterfire battle and other surface fires missions.

(g) The operational area visualization function enables improved SA. It uses tools that provide visualization of coordination measures, ingress and egress routes, and air defense threats. It also enables the commander and staff to visualize friendly fires in three dimensions over any area. Control and coordination measures also can be overlaid with imagery and terrain data to improve SA and planning.

(2) **Advanced Field Artillery Tactical Data System (AFATDS)**

(a) AFATDS is a fully automated C2 and communications system that prioritizes targets and pairs them with optimal fire support weapon systems. It gives commanders timely, accurate, and coordinated fire support to prioritize and engage targets. AFATDS can execute as a completely automated system, but allows for human intervention whenever necessary or at optional points. Configurable commanders' guidance is factored into each mission. Tailorable options and rule sets are available for target processing, weapon pairing, information distribution, and communications redundancy. AFATDS supports planning, execution, movement control, artillery mission support, FA fire direction operations, and target analysis and engagement.

(b) Unit relationships are user-configurable to adapt to changing needs and force structure. The system provides agility, allowing for the establishment of the sensor-to-shooter link while enforcing mission coordination requirements. AFATDS provides critical SA. Both friendly and enemy unit graphics are displayed, along with target information from multiple sources. Due to multilevel communications across the network, unit status and weapon platforms are monitored and updated continually on the map. Information may be directly accessed from the map symbols. Friendly and enemy units, targets, and operational areas can all be seen. Each AFATDS workstation may filter the information to be displayed, allowing the commander to monitor the dynamic current situation, missions processing through the system, and target updates from a unique perspective.

(c) AFATDS is not limited to FA communications, but can communicate and exchange data with Army, Air Force, Marine Corps, Navy, and North Atlantic Treaty Organization (NATO) systems. It is interoperable with all fires subsystems including gun display unit, artillery fire control systems, Firefinder Radar, Airborne Target Handover System, and forward observer (FO) system. It interoperates with the Army Battle Command Systems suite. The system also interoperates with joint level automated systems such as Tactical Airspace Integration System, TBMCS, Joint Surveillance and Target Attack Radar System (Ground Control Station), and Global Command and Control System, as well as with Allied FA C2 systems such as the United Kingdom's Battlefield Artillery Target Engagement System and the German ADLER. It operates over wire, combat net radio, mobile subscriber equipment, and satellite and can communicate over local area network for SECRET Internet Protocol Router Network (SIPRNET)/Non-Secure Internet Protocol Router Network (NIPRNET) and Enhanced Position Location and Reporting System operations.

(d) The planning function within AFATDS allows for detailed planning and COA analysis by projecting friendly and enemy positions, guidance specific to the plan, and a task organization for the plan. In order to assist with the planning function, an enemy template tool is provided. A system tool supports multiphase maneuver COAs and can compare and recommend the best COA considering commander's priorities. Plans can be easily disseminated. The planning activity does not affect the current situation until the operator implements the plan. Plans are implemented into the current situation by phase — this immediately updates the unit task organization guidance, geometry, and target database to reflect changes.

(e) Target analysis and engagement is a robust aspect of AFATDS. Target list management functions allow for copy and merge, target duplication checks, sorting, searching, and target data reception and transmission. Fire plans and schedules of fires guidance can also be applied to target analysis (e.g., target selection standards, HPTs, decay time, target prioritization). The fire support system task list alone can contain a 100-rule set of prioritized target to weapon system parings and a prioritized list of commander's preferences. Preplanned missions can be linked to sensor reports for dynamic targeting. The system can deal with many weapons and pair those weapons to targets, minimizing the sensor to shooter timeline. The system can filter sensor reports so that every report does not have to be engaged, and the system also selects the best weapon and munitions based on target parameters (e.g., environment, countermeasures, target location error [TLE], age), the munitions required (e.g., effects capability, hazard area), and weapon status (e.g., response time, current mission load, ammunition inventory). AFATDS can determine quantities of munitions to achieve a desired target damage effects. The system will filter targets and process missions based on a configurable mission value and precedence. The system analyzes cannon, mortar, rocket, ATACMS, fixed- and rotary-wing air, naval gun, standard missile, and Tomahawk as possibilities for weapons. It deconflicts ground and airspace encroachments (spatial coordination is four dimensional, including time analysis), is fully automatic, and keeps interested nodes appraised of targeting information. The system considers commanders' guidance, latest unit status, mission history, and effects algorithms, which determine munition quantity for both guided and unguided munitions. During mission processing, the operator may view and tailor the system recommendation. The intervention display shows all key data and analysis results.

(3) **Theater Battle Management Core System**

(a) The TBMCS is a force level integrated air C2 system. TBMCS provides hardware, software, and communications interfaces to support the preparation, modification, and dissemination of the force-level air battle plan (ABP). The ABP includes the ATO and airspace control order (ACO). TBMCS unit-level operations and intelligence applications provide Air Force wings the capability to receive the ABP, parse it, and manage wing operations and intelligence to support execution of the ABP.

(b) TBMCS supports the development and sharing of a common relevant operational picture of theater air and surface activity. Common TBMCS applications and interfaces provide a network for joint force data sharing. The TBMCS intelligence and targeting applications at the theater JFACC level, at the ASOC, and at the DASC support the coordination of precision engagement fires, safe passage zones, and near real-time warnings of impending air attack. The air and surface surveillance and weapons coordination engagement options enable synchronized operations and employment of the correct weapons for each target to generate the desired results. Engagement intentions and results assessments are shared by all TBMCS network participants, contributing to improved decisionmaking by commanders.

(c) TBMCS links tactical aviation and related units to the JFACC. When properly employed, TBMCS is a tool enabling linkage from the operational objectives of the commander, joint task force, through the JFACC, to the tactical activity of individual units. It also facilitates air battle planning, intelligence, operations, and execution functions for theater air operations; and enables coordination among higher, adjacent, and subordinate units and across Service boundaries.

(d) TBMCS fielding includes every theater air component, all Navy aircraft carriers and command ships, all Marine air wings, and all Air Force flying wings and ASOC squadrons. Army BCDs also interface with TBMCS. TBMCS uses two primary databases: the air operations database and the Modernized Integrated Database (MIDB). TBMCS contains a combination of processes and tools to support ATO production, which is the primary product TBMCS.

(4) **Airborne Warning and Control System.** The AWACS provides radar control and surveillance of air traffic. The AWACS's range, flexibility, and C2 system capabilities enable it to operate directly subordinate to the JAOC. It is able to provide many of the capabilities of the CRC, depending upon mission configuration and the needs of the theater. It can establish data links with other C2 nodes, such as the ASOC, and can disseminate air defense warnings and an accurate air picture. AWACS can also provide limited functions of the ASOC and TAC(A). AWACS cannot provide positive CID of ground targets.

(5) **Joint Surveillance Target Attack Radar System (JSTARS).** JSTARS performs theater-wide C2 and ISR support missions. JSTARS provides radar surveillance and targeting information to component commanders to develop an understanding of the enemy situation and to support operations. JSTARS mission capabilities contribute to an understanding of the friendly and enemy situation and assist ground, air, and naval commanders in delaying, disrupting, and destroying enemy forces and C2 of friendly forces, in accordance with the JFC's overall objectives. JSTARS supports these component operations by providing continuous wide area surveillance and targeting support to commanders equipped with common ground station and Joint Service Work Station. JSTARS can also support air operations to include AI, CAS, offensive counterair, and nontraditional missions. JSTARS can also provide limited functions of the ASOC and TAC(A). JSTARS cannot provide positive CID of ground targets.

(6) **Unmanned Aircraft Systems (UASs).** UASs offer the joint force significant capabilities and are integrated into all levels by the Services. UASs can be employed for higher risk and longer endurance missions with varying levels of autonomy and survivability because they have no aircrew design limitations. As an ISR platform, a UAS can provide timely ISR required for attacking and assessing targets (e.g., TSTs, HPTs, and HVTs). They offer a broad range of collection capabilities, including communications intelligence, electronic intelligence, electro-optical, infrared imagery, and real-time imagery. In addition, a UAS can provide target marking, laser designation, communications gateway extension (e.g., communications relay, network extension), ordnance delivery, and weapons effects assessment in support of joint fire support (see Chapter III, "Joint Fire Support Planning and Execution," subparagraph 7a[3], "Unmanned Aircraft Systems"). In all of these capacities, UAS provide the JFC with options that have significant risk management advantages, such as persistence and minimal risk to friendly personnel, over manned systems.

(7) **Service Assets.** Each Service operates additional assets such as the US Army's Airborne Reconnaissance Low-Multifunction, the US Navy's EP-3s, or the US Air Force's RC-135s and U-2s that, if allocated or used in a net-centric reporting environment, can also provide timely intelligence support to joint fire support.

CHAPTER III
JOINT FIRE SUPPORT PLANNING AND EXECUTION

> *"Commanders and leaders must remain flexible and therefore, must keep plans simple. Be nimble of mind."*
>
> **General Shalikashvili, Chairman of the Joint Chiefs of Staff (1993-1997), quoted at Ft. Polk**

1. Introduction

This chapter focuses on the planning and coordination of joint fire support. Joint fire support planning and coordination ensures that all available joint fire support is synchronized in accordance with the JFC's plan. **The key to effective integration of joint fire support is the thorough and continuous inclusion of all component fire support elements in the joint planning process, aggressive coordination efforts, and a vigorous execution of the plan.** Commanders should not rely solely on their joint fire support agencies to plan and coordinate joint fire support. A continuous dialogue between the commander, subordinate commanders, and joint fire support planners must occur.

a. Joint fire support planning is an integral part of the overall planning process. Joint fire support planners and/or coordinators actively participate with other members of the staff to develop estimates, give the commander recommendations, develop the joint fire support portion of the CONOPS, and supervise the execution of the commander's decision. The effectiveness of their planning and coordination is predicated on the commander providing clear and precise guidance.

b. **All components can plan for and coordinate joint fire support.** Integral to the commander's CONOPS is the concept of fires. Just as the JFC's intent and CONOPS should take into account the integration and synchronization of tactical, operational, and strategic operations, the CONOPS for component commanders should integrate and synchronize joint fire support at the tactical as well as the operational level. Joint fire support planning and coordination must be continuous and its execution decentralized.

See JP 3-0, Joint Operations, and JP 5-0, Joint Operation Planning, for a more detailed discussion of planning and operational considerations.

2. Joint Fire Support Planning

The purpose of joint fire support planning is to optimize its employment by integrating and synchronizing joint fire support with the commander's maneuver plan. **During the planning phase, commanders develop a CONOPS, including the concept for fires. Commanders determine how to shape the operational environment with fires to assist maneuver and how to use maneuver to exploit the use of joint fire support.** Objectives are restated in terms of what effects are required from joint fire support. Decisive operations, freedom of action, massing the effects of firepower, and depth and simultaneity are typical considerations. Joint fire support planners are responsible for advising commanders on the best use of available joint fires support, developing joint fire support plans, issuing necessary orders in the name of appropriate commanders, and implementing approved joint fire support plans for the component or joint force. Joint fire support requirements are considered throughout the JFC's planning and decision-making processes and during all phases of an operation.

a. **Planning.** Contingency planning of joint fire support is a complex task. Joint fire support planning becomes even more complex during crisis action planning due to the limited time to plan and coordinate operations that may require rapid execution. During crisis situations, joint fire support planning must expeditiously organize and prioritize limited assets to synchronize fires.

b. **Basic Joint Fire Support Tasks.** Effectiveness of the joint fire support effort is measured by creating desired effects on the enemy, setting conditions for decisive operations, and supporting joint force operations. **Effective joint fire support depends on planning for the successful performance of the following four basic fire support tasks:**

(1) **Support Forces in Contact.** The commander must provide responsive joint fire support that protects and ensures freedom of maneuver to forces in contact with the enemy throughout the operational area.

(2) **Support the Concept of Operation.** The CONOPS clearly and concisely expresses what the JFC intends to accomplish and how it will be done using available resources. The concept of fires must describe how joint fires will be synchronized and integrated to support the JFC's objectives as articulated in the CONOPS.

(3) **Synchronize Joint Fire Support.** Joint fire support is synchronized through fire support coordination, beginning with the commander's estimate and CONOPS. Joint fire support must be planned both continuously and concurrently with the development of the scheme of maneuver. Further, operations providing joint fire support must be synchronized with other joint force operations (e.g., air operations, cyberspace operations, ISR functions, SO, and IO) in order to optimize the application of limited resources, achieve synergy, and avoid fratricide.

(4) **Sustain Joint Fire Support Operations.** Joint fire support planners must formulate joint fire support plans to reflect logistic limitations and to exploit logistic capabilities. Ammunition, fuel, food, water, maintenance, transportation, and medical support are all critical to sustaining joint fire support operations.

c. **Planning Considerations Across the Range of Military Operations**

(1) **Major Operations and Campaigns**

(a) To achieve national strategic objectives or protect national interests, the US national leadership may decide to conduct a major operation involving large-scale combat, placing the United States in a wartime state. In such cases, the goal is to **prevail** against the enemy as quickly as possible, conclude hostilities, and establish conditions favorable to the United States, the host nation, and its multinational partners.

(b) Major operations and campaigns are complex and require detailed planning. Joint fire support for major operations may include, but is not limited to, the lethal effects of air support by manned and unmanned aircraft, NSFS, artillery, mortars, rockets, and missiles, as well as nonlethal effects from EA, CNA, and other nonlethal capabilities.

(c) Major operations and campaigns involve an ever-changing balance of offensive, defensive, and stability operations throughout all phases of the operation. Stability operations are missions, tasks, and activities that seek to maintain or reestablish a safe and secure environment and provide essential governmental services, emergency infrastructure reconstruction, or humanitarian relief. As the mission in stability operations is to restore vital national services, rather than destruction of an enemy force, the ROE will normally limit the level of lethal fires employed in support of these activities. Additionally, planners must consider the impact of joint fires on stability efforts throughout the operation; this includes the impacts of fires conducted during the early combat phases on later stabilization and reconstruction phases of the operation.

(2) **Crisis Response and Limited Contingency Operations**

(a) Crisis response and contingency operations can be a single small-scale, limited-duration operation or a significant part of a major operation of extended duration involving combat. The associated general strategic and operational objectives are to protect US interests and/or prevent surprise attack or further conflict.

(b) Joint fire support employed in support of crisis response and contingency operations may be the same as those employed for major operations and campaigns but are normally more restrictive in their application.

(3) **Military Engagement, Security Cooperation, and Deterrence**

(a) Military engagement, security cooperation, and deterrence operations encompass a wide range of activities where the military instrument of national power is tasked to support other government agencies (OGAs) and cooperate with intergovernmental organizations (IGOs), such as the United Nations or NATO, and other countries to protect and enhance national security interests and deter conflict. These operations usually involve a combination of conventional and unconventional forces and capabilities as well as the efforts of OGAs, IGOs, and nongovernmental organizations (NGOs) in a complementary fashion.

(b) Various joint operations, such as a show of force or enforcement of sanctions, support deterrence by demonstrating national resolve and willingness to use force when necessary. Others, such as humanitarian and civic assistance programs, promote international stability by enhancing a climate of peaceful cooperation.

(c) Lethal joint fire support employed in support of security cooperation and deterrence operations are normally the most restrictive in their application and may be limited to defensive fires only.

3. **Other Planning Considerations**

a. **Intelligence, Surveillance, and Reconnaissance.** Limited ISR assets that will be in high demand by numerous entities, make it imperative that fire support planners carefully consider their ISR requirements and closely coordinate with ISR planners. Target and munition selection, mitigation of collateral damage, and assessment cannot be accomplished without accurate and timely ISR support.

b. **Terminal Guidance Operations**

(1) TGO are those actions that provide electronic, mechanical, voice, or visual communications that provide approaching aircraft and/or weapons additional information regarding a specific target location. Various ground elements or aircrews conducting a wide variety of missions can search for, identify, and provide the location of targets using systems like Global Positioning System (GPS), laser designators/range finders, aircraft targeting pods, etc. Unless qualified as a JTAC or FAC(A), personnel conducting TGO do not have the authority to grant weapons release to attacking aircraft. These functions must be done by appropriate C2 authorities or a JTAC/FAC(A).

Note. Terminal guidance is guidance applied to a weapon between midcourse guidance and arrival in the vicinity of the target and may be a function of TGO, CAS, interdiction, or other missions.

(a) TGO can be used to facilitate attacks on targets in locations where the supported commander determines that the distance from friendly forces to the target is adequate to preclude the need for a JTAC or FAC(A) to perform detailed integration of each air mission with the fire and movement of friendly forces.

(b) TGO independent of CAS (not in close proximity to friendly forces) requires personnel conducting TGO to have direct or indirect communications with the individual operating/commanding the delivery system, plus connectivity with TGO weapons release authority.

(2) For TGO to be successful, C2 is essential; ACMs and radio procedures need to be established and understood by all participating units and aircrew. TGO may leverage CAS, TST, or other tactics, techniques, and procedures to aid in execution (such

as the CAS nine-line briefing format), but **TGO should not be confused with CAS operations requiring detailed integration performed by a qualified JTAC or FAC(A) in close proximity to friendly forces.**

c. **Acquisition of Targets**

(1) Laser designator and coordinate seeking weapons (CSW) acquisition devices can enhance current capabilities of artillery, NSFS, and aircraft in the delivery of munitions. Both aircraft (manned and unmanned) platforms and ground based observers can laser-designate targets for laser-guided weapons and provide precision coordinates for CSW. Employment of lasers can provide fire support personnel with precise target marking, enhanced visual TA, and surprise. It can also reduce the weapon and/or sortie attack requirements. However, several factors — environment, laser system inherent limits, target types, and laser code management — affect laser employment. Joint fire support planners and fire support coordinators must understand advantages and limitations when employing lasers. Additional guidance can be found in Appendix C, "Laser-Guided Systems," and JP 3-09.3, *Close Air Support).*

(2) Planning for using CSW assets in major combat operations carries significant implications for intelligence resources. Given the high volume of targets in the early days of an operation, advance preparation of targeting solutions will be essential for meeting commanders' guidance for target effects and ROE for collateral damage minimization. Just as target systems analysis is crucial to identify vulnerabilities for attack, the concept of "aimpoint development" must be applied to optimize and coordinate the precise effects achievable with CSW employment.

(3) Aimpoint development involves interactive application of point mensuration, weaponeering, and collateral damage estimation (CDE). This, in turn, requires suitably skilled target analysts using integrated toolsets to reduce human pointing and transcribing errors. Saving mensurated points into the MIDB requires individual operator certification as prescribed in Chairman of the Joint Chiefs of Staff Instruction (CJCSI) 3505.01A, *Target Coordinate Mensuration Certification and Program Accreditation.* In addition, significant workload is involved in deriving mensurated coordinates, weaponeering, and performing CDE for each joint desired point of impact data set as defined in Defense Intelligence Agency Instruction 3000.002, *US/Allied Target Analysis Program.*

d. **Nuclear Fires Planning.** Joint nuclear fires are collaboratively planned by US Strategic Command (USSTRATCOM) in support of the JFC's efforts in accordance with guidance supplied in overarching policies such as the Joint Strategic Capabilities Plan (JSCP) and JSCP-Nuclear. Planning efforts are differentiated as either strategic planning or theater planning. Only the President of the United States may authorize the employment of nuclear weapons through the Commander, USSTRATCOM. Specific execution details and operational procedures can be found in USSTRATCOM's Global Strike Plan and Emergency Action Procedures.

e. **Consequence of Execution Planning.** When targeting enemy weapons of mass destruction (WMD) storage sites, weapon systems, or production facilities, the fires cell must complete detailed consequence of execution planning to determine the potential release hazards due to the strike. Ground commanders in the target area must be advised of the predicted hazard area and must be given enough time to take appropriate force protection measures. Effects on the local civilians must be anticipated and planned for as well. This planning must be done not only for WMD sites, but also for targets known or suspected to contain toxic industrial chemicals or materials.

f. **Multinational Considerations**

(1) Military operations will normally be joint and often multinational. Fire support coordination in multinational operations demands special arrangements with multinational forces and local authorities. To maximize the fires of the multinational force and to minimize the possibility of fratricide, the multinational force commander and staff become familiar with each nation's capabilities and limitations in munitions, digital capability, and training. This also enhances the capability to conduct fire support coordination throughout the multinational force. These special arrangements include communications and language requirements, liaison personnel, and interoperability procedures. A standard operating procedure (SOP) should be established for fire support to achieve the most effective results for its use by the multinational force. To maximize the effectiveness of fire support, the multinational force staff performs the following:

(a) Integrate joint and multinational systems and procedures to determine priorities, and identify and track targets.

(b) Identify delivery systems.

(c) Assess post-attack results.

(d) Clear fires.

(e) Plan and coordinate the use of FSCMs.

(2) Examples of coordinated fire support arrangements:

(a) Establish NATO standardization agreements (STANAGs). These provide participants with common terminology and procedures. When operating with countries not in NATO, similar SOP agreements must be made.

(b) Use SOF teams assigned to multinational units to provide the JFC an accurate evaluation of capabilities, location, and activities of multinational forces, thus facilitating the JFC's C2.

(c) Establish guidelines for clearance of indirect fires in the ROE. See JP 3-16, *Multinational Operations*, for further information.

(d) Use a standard datum.

(e) Establish common meteorological procedures and standards.

(f) Provide liaison officers as required.

(g) Establish/coordinate the multinational ROE before beginning hostilities, and continually refine them during operations.

(h) Establish the policy for indirect fire systems using non-precision munitions within the ROE.

(i) Establish the policy for using smoke, illumination, and cluster munitions with inherent high dud potential within the ROE.

(j) Establish SOPs for how digitally and non-digitally equipped forces operate together. When automatic interfaces are unworkable, determine liaison officer requirements.

(k) Establish a multinational target numbering system.

4. **Joint Fire Support Planning Process**

a. **Introduction.** Joint fire support planning is accomplished utilizing both the targeting and joint fire support estimate processes. It is a continual and cyclical process of planning, synchronizing, executing, and assessing joint fires involving tactical, operational, and strategic considerations that also utilizes joint fire support communications systems and architectures. Initiated during mission analysis and continuing through post-execution assessment, the joint fire support planning process includes the following steps: end state and the commander's objectives; target development and prioritization; capabilities analysis; commander's decision and force assignment; mission planning and force execution; and assessment (see Figure III-1).

More detailed information on this and related processes can be found in JP 3-60, Joint Targeting, *and the* United States Joint Forces Command (USJFCOM) Joint Fires and Targeting Handbook.

(1) The JFC and component commander staffs synchronize joint fire support operations to optimize effects in time, space, and purpose to produce maximum relative combat power at a decisive place and time. To facilitate synchronization efforts, commanders and staffs must have a thorough knowledge of joint and Service doctrine, major system capabilities, and procedures.

(2) Joint fires and fire support are coordinated and synchronized through the joint targeting cycle. The purpose of targeting is to integrate and synchronize fires into joint operations. Targeting also supports the process of linking the desired effects of fires

their scheme of maneuver and show how it supports the JTF CONOPS and works within targeting guidance, prior to the JIPTL review. This effort allows both component and joint fires to be deconflicted, coordinated, and synchronized.

b. **Targeting**

(1) Most JFC and component requirements for joint fire support are planned and executed using the joint targeting process. The purpose of targeting is to integrate and synchronize fires into joint operations. Targeting is the process of selecting and prioritizing targets and matching the appropriate response to them, considering operational requirements and capabilities. The targeting cycle is a rational and iterative process that methodically analyzes, prioritizes, and assigns assets against targets systematically to create those effects that will contribute to the achievement of the JFC's objectives. It also supports the process of linking the desired effects of fires to actions and tasks at the joint force component level.

(2) Within military operations, targeting must be focused on creating specific effects to achieve the JFC's objectives or the subordinate component commander's supporting objectives. Targeting proceeds from the definition of the problem to an assessment of the results achieved by the executed COAs. The process allows for the testing of multiple solution paths, a thorough understanding of the problem, and the refinement of proposed solutions. The joint targeting process is flexible and adaptable to a wide range of circumstances.

Detailed information on targeting can be found in JP 3-60, Joint Targeting.

c. **Component Planning Steps.** This process consists of **a series of interrelated steps**, requiring joint force staff and component cross coordination throughout.

(1) **Receipt of Mission.** Upon receipt of a mission, joint fire support personnel assist the commander in mission analysis. Joint fire support personnel must understand the commander's guidance on the following:

(a) Specific COAs.

(b) Objectives and end state.

(c) ISR.

(d) TSTs, HVTs, and HPTs.

(e) Use of weapons effects and special munitions such as blast, fragmentation, cluster, nuclear, mines, and lasers.

(f) Acceptable risks.

(g) C2.

(h) Commitment of the reserve force.

(i) Critical events to be considered.

(j) Commander's assumptions.

(k) ROE.

(l) Assessment.

(m) Host nation concerns.

(2) **Target Analysis.** The commander establishes targeting guidance that must be incorporated into the joint fire support planning process. The commander establishes the priorities and describes the importance of a target set and/or category in relation to a given situation or phase of operation. During an air assault operation, for example, attacking known enemy air defense systems may be more important than attacking enemy artillery sites. Targeting tactics, techniques, and procedures are discussed in JP 3-60, *Joint Targeting*. The overall effectiveness and efficiency of the joint fire support planning process increases as leaders consider the following:

(a) The type and amount of delivery assets and munitions available.

(b) The effectiveness of weapon system and/or munitions.

(c) The size, type, ability to detect, and posture of the target.

(d) Joint fire support asset characteristics (range, accuracy, rate of fire, and response time).

(e) Civilians and damage to civilian objects.

(f) Target selection standards and decision criteria for target reattack.

(g) Damage criteria.

(3) **Preparing the Joint Fire Support Estimate. Typically component staffs employ the use of a joint fire support estimate.** This estimate influences how available joint fire support resources are employed to support the possible COAs and helps joint fire support planners and/or coordinators integrate and synchronize the employment of joint fire support resources. **The estimate is a realistic appraisal of the effort required to support the operation.** It serves as a basis for identifying joint fire support priority requirements that support the commander's intent. Factors that could affect the mission and may be considered in the joint fire support estimate include the following:

(a) The task organization of subordinate forces and their missions.

(b) The availability of joint fire support resources, including FA, CAS (by both fixed- and rotary-wing aircraft), NSFS, SOF, EW, and ISR assets.

(c) The probable enemy fires plan.

(d) Enemy fires capability.

(e) The identification of TSTs, HVTs, and HPTs.

(f) Consumption factors (type and quantity), positioning requirements, and priority of logistic support.

(g) Joint fires-related decision points.

(4) **Issuing the Commander's Estimate.** Based on information provided in the staff estimates, the commander issues an estimate. It should provide joint fire support planners and/or coordinators with guidance regarding prioritization of targets, desired effects, and reattack.

(5) **Course of Action Analysis.** COA analysis is a systematic review process performed by a commander and staff to determine the best COA for a given operation. Each COA must be analyzed to consider the implications of both friendly and enemy options during an operation. Joint fire support planners and/or coordinators are key players in this analysis process. They advise the commanders on the joint fire support assets available and recommend the most effective use of these assets. As the analysis progresses, joint fire support planners and/or coordinators continuously evaluate the integration of joint fire support into the commander's emerging concept of operation, to include branches and sequels. As a result of this interaction, the commander's options are influenced by the availability and allocation of joint fire support assets. The finished product of this analysis is a COA that integrates joint fire support with maneuver and synchronizes operations. Joint fire support planners use the results of COA development in the targeting process.

(6) **Initiating Planning Actions.** Once the commander decides on a COA, joint staff and fire support planners:

(a) Refine named areas of interest, decision points, and HVTs/HPTs.

(b) Integrate and refine the collection, TA, and assessment plan. All collection assets are tasked and integrated to ensure there are no gaps in the coverage of the AO.

(c) Develop joint fire support tasks, responsibilities, and requirements.

(d) Develop the joint fires employment concept and joint fire support plan.

d. **The Joint Fire Support Plan.** See Appendix B, "Joint Fire Support Operation Order Format," for an example format.

5. **Joint Fire Support Coordination**

a. Joint fire support coordination includes all efforts to deconflict attacks, avoid fratricide, reduce duplication of effort, and assist in shaping the operational environment. **Coordination procedures must be flexible and responsive to the ever-changing dynamics of warfighting.** Simplified arrangements for approval or concurrence should be established. Coordination is reflected in the CONOPS and in the sequencing and timing of actions to achieve objectives. Coordination is enhanced when joint fire support personnel clearly understand the commander's intent. A very important part of the coordination process is the identification of potential fratricide situations and the necessary coordination measures to positively manage and control the attack of targets.

(1) **Synchronization.** Joint fire support coordination is a flexible process that must be kept as simple as possible to produce the desired results. The JFC and component commanders **synchronize joint fire support operations to place the right attack means on the correct target at the precise time.** To achieve synchronization, commanders and staffs must have a thorough knowledge of each Service's doctrine, major systems, significant capabilities and limitations, and often their tactics, techniques, and procedures.

(2) **Principles.** Agencies involved in coordinating joint fire support employ several principles. These principles are extensions of the four basic fire support tasks discussed earlier in this chapter.

(a) **Plan Early and Continuously.** To effectively integrate joint fire support with the scheme of maneuver, planning must begin when the commander states the mission and provides the command guidance. Whenever commander's guidance is needed during planning, joint fire support planners and/or coordinators should solicit that guidance from the commander. Planning is continuous and keeps pace with the dynamics of the battle. Whenever possible, direct coordination can increase the probability for success. The tactical unit providing the support should contact the unit being supported to conduct detailed tactical planning. This is especially important, and often the hardest to execute, when the support is being provided across component boundaries such as during CAS.

(b) **Ensure Continuous Flow of Targeting Information.** Joint fire support planners and/or coordinators should ensure that TA requirements for joint fire support are identified and focused on detecting priority targets. Staffs ensure that target information from all sources is evaluated and routed to the appropriate attack means. This includes information from all echelons and from adjacent and supporting elements.

(c) **Consider the Use of all Lethal and/or Nonlethal Attack Means.** Joint fire support planners and/or coordinators consider all attack means available at their level and higher levels. They also consider the command guidance for the use of these attack means in the present battle and in future battles.

(d) **Use the Lowest Echelon Capable of Furnishing Effective Support.** In order to keep joint fire support responsive, the **lowest level having effective means available should deliver it.** Joint fire support planners and/or coordinators must determine what is needed. If assets are inadequate, they must request additional joint fire support from the appropriate echelon or component. Coordination among Service and functional components should occur at the lowest possible echelon. When coordination cannot be accomplished or additional guidance is required, the next higher echelon should be consulted.

(e) **Furnish the Type of Joint Fire Support Requested.** The requester is usually in the best position to determine joint fire support requirements. However, joint fire support planners and/or coordinators are in a position to weigh the request against the commander's guidance on priority targets and the current and future needs for joint fire support. The component, unit, or organization providing the fire support is normally best able to provide the detailed targeting planning for optimum results.

(f) **Use the Most Effective Joint Fire Support Means.** Requests for joint fire support are transmitted to the force capable of delivering the most effective joint fires within the required time. When developing a recommendation for the appropriate weapon system, **the joint fire support planners and/or coordinators should consider the nature and importance of the target, the engagement time window, the availability of attack assets, and the results desired.** In some circumstances, it may be necessary to sequence the attack by fixing the enemy with immediately available joint fire support assets, while coordinating a subsequent more detailed attack by more effective assets. It may be necessary to use multiple assets to create the desired effects on a target.

(g) **Avoid Unnecessary Duplication.** A key task for joint fire support planners and/or coordinators is to ensure that duplications of joint fire support are resolved.

(h) **Coordinate Airspace**

<u>1</u>. All component commanders must have the freedom to use airspace to achieve the JFC's objectives and must have maximum flexibility to use assets (organic and joint) within that airspace. **Effective airspace management requires a responsive airspace control system, standardization, minimal restrictions, and continuous coordination among all airspace users.** Joint planning and coordination are necessary to minimize mutual interference while deploying and employing air defense and fire support assets.

See JP 3-52, Joint Airspace Control, *and JP 3-30,* Command and Control for Joint Air Operations, *for additional information.*

<u>2.</u> **Commanders, assisted by joint fire support planners and/or coordinators, must ensure that conflicts between surface-based indirect fire and air operations are minimized.** For example, an uncoordinated attack deep into the surface AO by the joint force land component could result in an unexpected repositioning of enemy air defense just prior to a planned air strike. Similarly, an uncoordinated air mission beyond the FSCL could influence the wrong enemy force and interfere with the ground scheme of maneuver.

<u>3.</u> **All Services operate systems for airspace control.** When similar Service systems are linked with the airspace control authority by communications, standardized procedures, and liaison, they become part of the integrated airspace control system. The highest probability of interference between aircraft and surface-to-surface weapons occurs at relatively low altitudes in the immediate vicinity of firing locations and target impact areas. FSCMs and ACMs exist within a network of component joint FISTs, liaison parties, and fire coordination elements. Using FSCMs and ACMs correctly can prevent fratricide and duplication of effort while increasing the effectiveness of air-to-ground and ground-to-ground ordnance.

JP 3-52, Joint Airspace Control, *contains a detailed discussion on airspace control.*

(i) **Provide Adequate Support.** The mission and commander's guidance determine the amount and type of joint fire support needed for success. **Joint fire support planners and/or coordinators** must inform the maneuver commander when joint fire support requirements exceed capabilities.

(j) **Provide for Rapid Coordination. Commanders must establish procedures and responsibilities for the rapid coordination of joint fire support.** In some circumstances, coordination of joint fire support will be detailed and done in advance. In other instances, due to operational circumstances, coordination will be rapid and less detailed. Poor communication and collaboration procedures or inadequate FSCMs may delay the delivery of joint fires, or the clearance of those fires, and jeopardize the force. Joint fire support planners and/or coordinators must know the availability of assets, the CONOPS, the commander's intent, FSCMs in effect, ROE, clearance of joint fires procedures, and any other restrictions.

(k) **Protect the Force.** Given the complexity inherent in joint fire support, **prevention of fratricide must always be a high priority.** Commanders at all levels must consciously and deliberately reduce the potential for fratricide.

<u>1.</u> In the execution of joint fire support, joint forces must implement measures to reduce the risk of fratricide to include disciplined execution of OPORDs, the ACO, depth, vertical and horizontal coordination among forces, CID procedures, and detailed situation awareness.

<u>2.</u> The change of established FSCMs and/or ACMs must be coordinated as far in advance as possible. All joint force coordinating agencies must inform their forces of the effective times and locations of new FSCMs and/or ACMs. Following direction to execute the change, the component operations cells should confirm the changes to ensure that affected forces are aware of new FSCM and/or ACM locations and that associated positive control measures are being followed.

<u>3.</u> Additional measures that may be considered to protect the force include:

<u>a.</u> Guidance and restrictions governing the authority, use, reporting, marking, and clearing of mines and munitions with high sub-munitions dud rates.

<u>b.</u> Restrictions on the use of incendiary munitions where resulting fires might endanger maneuvering forces.

<u>c.</u> Guidance regarding cessation of NSFS to ensure safety of amphibious shipping and joint forces operating in the AOA.

<u>d.</u> Policy on use of selected munitions and fuzes (e.g., variable time fuze) in the JOA and/or AO.

<u>e.</u> Development and disciplined use of common operational graphics and associated maneuver and ACMs and FSCMs throughout the joint force.

<u>f.</u> Special safety precautions to be observed during ship-to-shore movement and with operations involving helicopterborne assaults.

<u>g.</u> Weapons employment restrictions.

<u>h.</u> Target identification and engagement criteria.

<u>i.</u> Prohibited targets.

(l) **Analyze Effectiveness.** During an operation, the effectiveness of joint fire support is continuously evaluated to ensure that it is achieving the commander's intent.

(m) **Provide for Flexibility.** Joint fire support planners and/or coordinators must anticipate and provide for future contingencies. On-order missions and the careful positioning of assets give the commander the flexibility to respond to changing battlefield conditions.

b. **Control and Coordination Measures.** Within their operational areas, land and maritime commanders employ permissive and restrictive FSCMs to expedite attack of targets; protect forces, populations, critical infrastructure, and sites of religious or cultural significance; clear joint fires; deconflict joint fire support operations; and establish conditions for future operations. Along with other control measures, FSCMs and their associated procedures help ensure that joint fire support does not jeopardize troop safety, interfere with other attack means, or disrupt operations of adjacent subordinate units. Maneuver commanders position and adjust control measures consistent with the location of friendly forces, the concept of the operation, anticipated enemy actions, and in consultation with superior, subordinate, supporting, and affected commanders. The primary purpose of permissive measures is to facilitate the attack of targets. Permissive measures facilitate reducing or eliminating coordination requirements for the engagement of targets with conventional means. Restrictive measures impose requirements for specific coordination before engagement of targets. Control and coordination measures are discussed in detail in Appendix A, "Control and Coordination Measures."

6. Joint Fire Support Assessment

Assessment is a continuous process that measures the overall effectiveness of employing joint force capabilities during military operations. The JFC and component commanders assess the operational environment and the progress of operations, and compare them to their initial vision and intent.

a. The assessment process begins during mission analysis, when the commander and staff consider what to measure and how to measure it to determine progress toward accomplishing a task, creating an effect, or achieving an objective, and continues throughout execution. Assessment actions and measures help commanders adjust operations and resources as required, determine when to execute branches and sequels, and make other critical decisions to ensure current and future operations remain aligned with the mission and end state.

b. Assessment is conducted at all levels of war. At the operational and strategic levels it is typically more wide-ranging than at the tactical level and uses measures of effectiveness that support strategic and operational mission accomplishment. Strategic- and operational-level assessment efforts concentrate on broader tasks, effects, objectives, and progress toward the end state. Tactical-level assessment typically uses measures of performance to evaluate task accomplishment. The results of tactical tasks are often physical in nature, but also can reflect the impact on specific functions and systems. Assessment of results at the tactical level helps commanders determine operational and strategic progress, so JFCs must have a comprehensive, integrated assessment plan that links assessment activities and measures at all levels.

c. At the tactical level, combat assessment (CA) encompasses many tactical-level assessment actions and has implications at the operational level as well. CA typically focuses on determining the results of weapons engagement (with both lethal and nonlethal capabilities), and thus is an important component of joint fires, joint fire support, and the joint targeting process. To conduct CA, it is important to fully understand the linkages between the targets and the JFC's objectives, targeting guidance, and desired effects. CA is composed of three related elements: battle damage assessment, munitions effectiveness assessment, and reattack recommendations or future targeting.

For more on assessment, refer to JP 3-0, Joint Operations, *JP 3-60*, Joint Targeting, *and the* USJFCOM Joint Fires and Targeting Handbook.

7. **Joint Fire Support and Force Capabilities**

a. **Lethal.** Following is a general discussion of lethal capabilities available to the JFC for joint fire support planning.

(1) **Fixed-Wing Aircraft.** The flexibility, range, speed, lethality, precision, and ability to mass at a desired time and place contributes significantly to the overall joint fire support available to a JFC. Fixed-wing aircraft offer the versatility and capability to deliver combat power against the enemy when and where needed to attain objectives across the range of military operations. The ability of aircraft to employ precision-guided munitions offers a distinct advantage over other weapon systems in many cases. Guided weapons can correct for ballistic, release, and targeting errors in flight. Manned aircraft can offer the advantage of providing immediate attack assessment. Also, stealth technology and the ability to employ air launched conventional standoff weaponry offer unique advantages and, in effect, may achieve their own local air superiority due to their reduced detectability.

(2) **Attack Helicopters.** The US Army normally employs attack helicopters as maneuver units capable of conducting two basic types of attack missions, close combat attack and interdiction attack. US Army attack helicopters can also perform CAS functions when operating in support of another component. The USMC employs its attack rotary-wing aviation primarily as a CAS platform. As an integral part of the MAGTF, the ACE deploys as a supporting element to the GCE to execute CAS missions in support of ground maneuver elements. Attack helicopters are capable of employing precision guided weapons and providing terminal guidance for other weapon platforms. They are also capable of operating during periods of limited visibility.

(3) **Unmanned Aircraft Systems.** The long endurance capability of UASs has demonstrated that UASs can be critical to the support of TST, HVT, and HPT missions. Situations may require UASs to support CAS, strike coordination and reconnaissance, AI, and other joint fires missions. Specific tasks for the UASs may include: target acquisition/marking, terminal guidance of ordnance, providing precision coordinates for GPS-aided munitions, delivery of onboard precision-guided ordnance, battle damage assessment, and retargeting (i.e., shoot-look-shoot). In the TST role, UASs are routed, controlled, and deconflicted in the same manner as fixed- and rotary-winged manned aircraft, as outlined in joint doctrine. Current weapons employed by unmanned aircraft are in the 500-pound class or less and are usually GPS- or laser-guided.

(4) **Missiles**

(a) ATACMS provides long-range, surface-to-surface fires against high value, well-defended targets, day or night, and in near-all weather conditions. The ATACMS missiles fired from the Multiple Launch Rocket System (MLRS) and the High Mobility Artillery Rocket System (HIMARS) launchers deliver warheads that include antipersonnel/antimateriel bomblets, unitary high-explosive charges, or guided submunitions. ATACMS can support a full range of operations including TSTs, J-SEAD, counterfires, and in strikes requiring high levels of accuracy. Their inherent low risk, accuracy, and range make these missiles a very viable option against stationary, non-hardened targets.

(b) US Navy TLAMs can be effective in engaging well-defended targets at long distances and provide a potent precision employment option to the joint force. Their inherent low risk, accuracy, and range make these missiles a very viable option against stationary, non-hardened targets. The TLAM weapon system may require coordination with the strike and mission planners in theater at the maritime component commander's HQ. Planning is an ongoing process, independent of the decision to use the weapon and can run in parallel to the decision process. With proper planning, TLAMs are capable of conducting short-notice employment, day or night, with few weather restrictions. TLAM strikes may be conducted without air support and/or when manned aircraft loss is considered to be likely. TLAMs are also capable of neutralizing enemy air defenses to facilitate a much larger attack by land- and maritime-based airpower. In theater, the associated afloat planning systems suites provide the joint force maritime component commander with the capability to plan new missions or modify selected missions in the operational area.

(c) The US Air Force conventional air-launched cruise missile (CALCM) is a near-precision, GPS-aided standoff weapon launched from a B-52. Mission planning for the CALCM is accomplished by reachback, and close coordination is required between missile planners, B-52 aircraft planners, and AOC planning staffs.

(d) The joint air-to-surface standoff missile (JASSM) is a US Air Force air launched, low observable (LO), subsonic cruise missile specifically designed to penetrate air defense systems. The missile incorporates GPS guidance with an infrared seeker in the terminal phase of flight. Optimizing JASSM's full precision and LO capabilities requires prior coordination with both strike units and target intelligence agencies.

(5) **Rockets.** The MLRS and the HIMARS launchers provide the joint force with effective counterfire and attack of enemy defenses, light materiel, and personnel targets. These weapon systems supplement cannon artillery fires by delivering large volumes of firepower against selected targets. The MLRS and HIMARS typically fire free-flight rockets against area targets and guided munitions against point targets. The guided MLRS rocket provides another precision attack capability to support maneuver forces and provide interdiction of HPTs and HVTs.

(6) **Cannon Artillery and Mortars.** Although cannon artillery and mortars primarily provide close supporting fires to maneuver forces, they can also perform other roles such as interdiction to support maneuver, or J-SEAD to facilitate air operations. New precision artillery rounds, such as the Excalibur, provide all weather precision strike capability for point targets in close proximity to friendly forces.

(7) **Naval Surface Fire Support**

(a) The general mission of NSFS ship units in an amphibious operation is to support the assault by destroying or neutralizing shore installations that oppose the approach of ships and aircraft, defenses that may oppose the LF, and defenses that may oppose the post-landing advance of the LF.

(b) When the number of ships permits, each assault battalion will be assigned a ship in DS. The DS mission establishes a one-to-one relationship between an NSFS ship and the supported unit. The ship delivers fires on planned targets and targets of opportunity in her zone of fire (ZF), which normally corresponds to the zone of action of the supported unit. When possible, ships capable of performing simultaneous missions will be given a DS mission to allow for maximum firepower to the forward units of the LF.

(c) The GS mission requires an NSFS ship to support the force as a whole or that portion of the force to which the ship is assigned. A ship in GS attacks targets in the ZF which corresponds to the zone of action of the supported unit. Prearranged fires are delivered in accordance with a schedule of fires published in the ATF OPORD and the NSFS plan in the LF OPORD. Fires may also be allocated to a subordinate unit for a specific mission(s). Upon completion of the mission(s), the ship reverts to GS. Ships in GS support regimental-sized units or larger.

For further details and information on lethal joint fires assets, see FM 3-09.32, Marine Corps Reference Publication (MCRP) 3-16.6B, Navy Tactics, Techniques, and Procedures (NTTP) 3-09.2, AFTTP(I) 3-2.6, J-FIRE, Multi-Service Procedures for the Joint Application of Firepower.

b. **Nonlethal.** Following is a general description of nonlethal capabilities available to the JFC that facilitate joint fire planning and support. It is important to note that nonlethal weapons are not without risk; but they are weapons explicitly designed and primarily employed so as to incapacitate personnel or materiel while minimizing fatalities, permanent injury to personnel, and undesired damage to property and the environment.

(1) **Information Operations.** The integration and synchronization of fires with IO through the targeting process is fundamental to creating the necessary synergy between IO and more traditional maneuver and strike operations. While all IO capabilities can be used in joint fire support, EA and CNA are discussed below.

(a) **Electronic Attack.** EA is the division of EW involving the use of electromagnetic (EM) energy, directed energy, or antiradiation weapons to attack personnel, facilities, or equipment with the intent of degrading, neutralizing, or destroying enemy combat capability and is considered a form of fires. EA includes: actions taken to prevent or reduce an enemy's effective use of the EM spectrum, such as jamming and EM deception, and employment of weapons that use either EM or directed energy as their primary destructive mechanism (e.g., lasers, radio frequency weapons, particle beams).

(b) **Computer Network Attack.** CNA is the division of computer network operations that uses computer networks to disrupt, deny, degrade, or destroy information resident in computers and computer networks, or the computers and networks themselves.

(2) **Other.** Other nonlethal joint fire support includes obscurant fires to mask friendly positions and illumination fires when required for night operations.

8. **Joint Fire Support Coordination Measures and Reference Systems**

a. **Fire Support Coordination Measures.** See Appendix A, "Control and Coordination Measures," for a detailed discussion of FSCMs.

b. **Global Area Reference System (GARS).** GARS provides commanders a worldwide common frame of reference for joint force SA to facilitate coordination, deconfliction, integration, and synchronization. For further guidance refer to JP 2-03, *Geospatial Intelligence Support to Joint Operations*.

9. **Combat Identification**

CID is the process of attaining an accurate characterization of detected objects in the operational environment sufficient to support an engagement decision. Depending on the situation and the operational decisions that must be made, this characterization may be limited to "friend," "enemy," "neutral," or "unknown." In other situations, other characterizations may be required — including, but not limited to, class, type, nationality, and mission configuration. CID characterizations, when applied with combatant commander ROE, enable engagement decisions and the subsequent use, or prohibition of use, of lethal and nonlethal weaponry to accomplish military objectives. CID is used for force posturing, C2, SA, and strike/no-strike employment decisions. Comprehensive CID training, in conjunction with effective CID procedures and available technology, can greatly reduce the risk of fratricide. Effective CID not only reduces the likelihood of fratricide, but also enhances joint fire support by instilling confidence that a designated target is, in fact, as described.

a. The JFC's CID procedures should be developed early during planning and ROE development. When developing the JFC's CID procedures, important considerations include the missions, capabilities, and limitations of all participants including multinational forces, OGAs, IGOs, and NGOs. There are many different CID procedures and systems currently in use by US and multinational forces. Experience has proven that early identification of common CID procedures significantly increases CID effectiveness.

b. CID-related information exchange orients on SA for friendly and neutral forces, restricted sites and structures, and identification of threat objects. During mission execution CID information requires constant coordination and should be conveyed to decisionmakers in an understandable manner.

10. Mitigation of Collateral Damage

a. Collateral damage is defined as, "The unintentional or incidental injury or damage to persons or objects that would not be lawful military targets in the circumstances ruling at the time." Such damage is not unlawful so long as it is not excessive in light of the overall military advantage anticipated from the attack. However, even though such fires may be lawful, commanders should ensure fires do not negatively impact operational or strategic objectives.

b. Under the law of armed conflict, the principle of proportionality requires that the anticipated loss of civilian life and damage to civilian property incidental to attacks must not be excessive in relation to the concrete and direct military advantage expected to be gained. **Commanders therefore have the responsibility to attempt to minimize collateral damage to the greatest extent practicable.** CDE is an important step in the target development process. However, it should not preclude the inclusion of valid military targets on a target list.

c. Target coordinate mensuration is a process for measurement of a feature or location on the earth to determine an absolute latitude, longitude, and height, and it is used in targeting to refer to the exact location of a target. Point mensuration has always been an important part of targeting, since the mensurated points represent the desired points of impact for the munitions employed. As the accuracy of weapons delivery has improved, the importance of mensuration has grown in proportion. When accomplished before ATO execution, it permits employment of an entire class of weapons (those, like GPS-aided and cruise missiles that guide to pre-set coordinates). This allows JAOC personnel to significantly shorten the dynamic targeting portion of the targeting process. Guided munitions guide to the mensurated point they are programmed to attack, so accurate mensuration is vital to their employment. However, mensuration is not required for accurate employment of all weapons.

d. WMD targets are a particular problem. Although the initial impact of a conventional munition on a WMD target may cause little collateral damage, secondary effects could include a release/dispersal of chemical, biological, or radiological material or even an imperfect detonation of a nuclear device. For this reason, WMD targets are usually placed on an RTL; however, mission priorities to combat WMD and/or military necessity may require JFCs to engage joint fires on WMD targets. JFCs should plan for follow-on operations to manage the consequences and mitigate the effects of collateral damage from WMD.

For more information on WMD, see JP 3-40, Joint Doctrine for Combating Weapons of Mass Destruction, *and JP 3-41,* Chemical, Biological, Radiological, Nuclear, and High-Yield Explosives Consequence Management.

e. In most operations, political or legal constraints require the creation of an NSL. These are locations with legally protected status, or that are placed off-limits to attack for important policy reasons.

f. **Collateral damage may be minimized through many different methods.** Choosing an appropriate weapons system, munition warhead, warhead fuzing, and final attack axis are all methods used to mitigate collateral damage.

g. As discussed earlier, nonlethal fires can be used to confuse, damage, deceive, delay, deny, disorganize, disrupt, influence, or locate the enemy. The development of nonlethal weapons has recently drawn greater interest due to the restraints imposed on using lethal fires and greater public sensitivity to military and civilian casualties. Accordingly, **JFCs and planners should seek joint fire support options that mitigate collateral damage and minimize noncombatant and/or civilian casualties, particularly in heavily populated areas.** The employment of nonlethal fires in supporting these operations will also be governed by their political impact.

For further information on mitigating collateral damage, see JP 3-60, Joint Targeting; *the methodology contained within CJCSI 3160.01,* No-Strike and the Collateral Damage Estimation Methodology; *and CJCSI 3122.06C,* Sensitive Target Approval and Review (STAR) Process.

APPENDIX A
CONTROL AND COORDINATION MEASURES

1. Fire Support Coordination Measures

Locations and implementing instructions for FSCMs are disseminated electronically by message, database update, and/or overlay through both command and joint fire support channels to higher, lower, and adjacent maneuver and supporting units. Typically they are further disseminated to each level of command, to include the establishing command and all concerned joint fire support agencies. Not all measures may apply to a joint operation. However, knowledge of the various FSCMs used by each component is necessary for the effective use of joint fire support.

a. **Planning and Coordination Considerations.** The establishment or change of an FSCM established by the JFLCC is typically initiated through the J-3 operations cell and ultimately approved by the JFC. FSCMs enhance the expeditious engagement of targets, protect forces, populations, critical infrastructure, and sites of religious or cultural significance, and set the stage for future operations. Commanders position and adjust FSCMs consistent with the operational situation and in consultation with superior, subordinate, supporting, and affected commanders. The operations cell informs coordination elements of the change and effective time. Conditions which dictate the change of FSCMs are also coordinated with the other agencies and components as appropriate. As conditions are met, the new FSCM effective time can be projected and announced. Following direction to execute the change, the operations cell should confirm with all liaison elements that the FSCM changes have been disseminated. This ensures that affected units are aware of new FSCM locations and associated positive control measures are being followed, thus reducing the risk of fratricide.

b. STANAG 2245, *Field Artillery and Fire Support Data Interoperability*, and STANAG 5620, *Standards for the Interoperability of Fire Support Automated Data Processing Systems*, are examples of international joint fire support agreements. Before commencing operations both joint force and component staff members must verify the status of FSCMs in a multinational operation.

c. Before discussing coordinating measures, a brief background on operational environment geometry will provide a better understanding for the application of the different types of FSCMs.

(1) Operational areas may be contiguous or noncontiguous. When they are contiguous, a boundary separates them and when noncontiguous, they do not share a boundary; the CONOPS links the elements of the force. Noncontiguous operational areas normally are characterized by a 360-degree boundary with the higher HQ responsible for the area between noncontiguous operational areas. Within both contiguous and noncontiguous areas, operations may be linear or nonlinear in nature.

(2) In linear operations, commanders direct and sustain combat power toward enemy forces in concert with adjacent units usually along lines of operations with identified forward lines of own troops (FLOTs). Emphasis is placed on maintaining the position of the land force in relation to other friendly forces usually resulting in contiguous operations where surface forces share boundaries. Linear operations are normally conducted against a deeply arrayed, echeloned enemy force or when the threat to lines of communication (LOCs) requires control of the terrain around those LOCs. In these circumstances, linear operations allow commanders to concentrate and integrate combat power more easily.

(3) In nonlinear operations, forces orient on objectives without geographic reference to adjacent forces and are usually characterized by more operations in noncontiguous areas. Nonlinear operations emphasize simultaneous operations along multiple lines of operation from selected bases. Nonlinear operations place a premium on intelligence, mobility, and sustainment.

See JP 3-0, Joint Operations, *for more on linear and nonlinear operations and contiguous and noncontiguous operational areas.*

2. **Permissive Measures**

    a. **Coordinated Fire Line**

    (1) **Purpose.** The coordinated fire line (CFL) is a line beyond which conventional indirect surface joint fire support means may fire at any time within the boundaries of the establishing HQ without additional coordination. The purpose of the CFL is to expedite the surface-to-surface engagement of targets beyond the CFL without coordination with the land commander in whose AO the targets are located.

    (2) **Establishment.** The CFL is usually established by a brigade or division commander equivalent, but it can also be established, especially in amphibious operations, by a maneuver battalion. It is located as close to the establishing unit as possible without interfering with the maneuver forces. There is no requirement for the CFL to be placed on identifiable terrain. However, additional considerations include the limits of ground observation, the location of the initial objectives in the offense, and the requirement for maximum flexibility in both maneuver and the delivery of supporting fires. Subordinate CFLs may be consolidated by higher HQ.

    (3) **Graphic Portrayal.** The CFL is graphically portrayed by a dashed black line, with "CFL" followed by the establishing HQ above the line and the effective date-time group (DTG) below the line (see Figure A-1).

    b. **Fire Support Coordination Line**

    (1) **Purpose.** FSCLs facilitate the expeditious engagement of targets of opportunity beyond the coordinating measure. An FSCL does not divide an AO. The

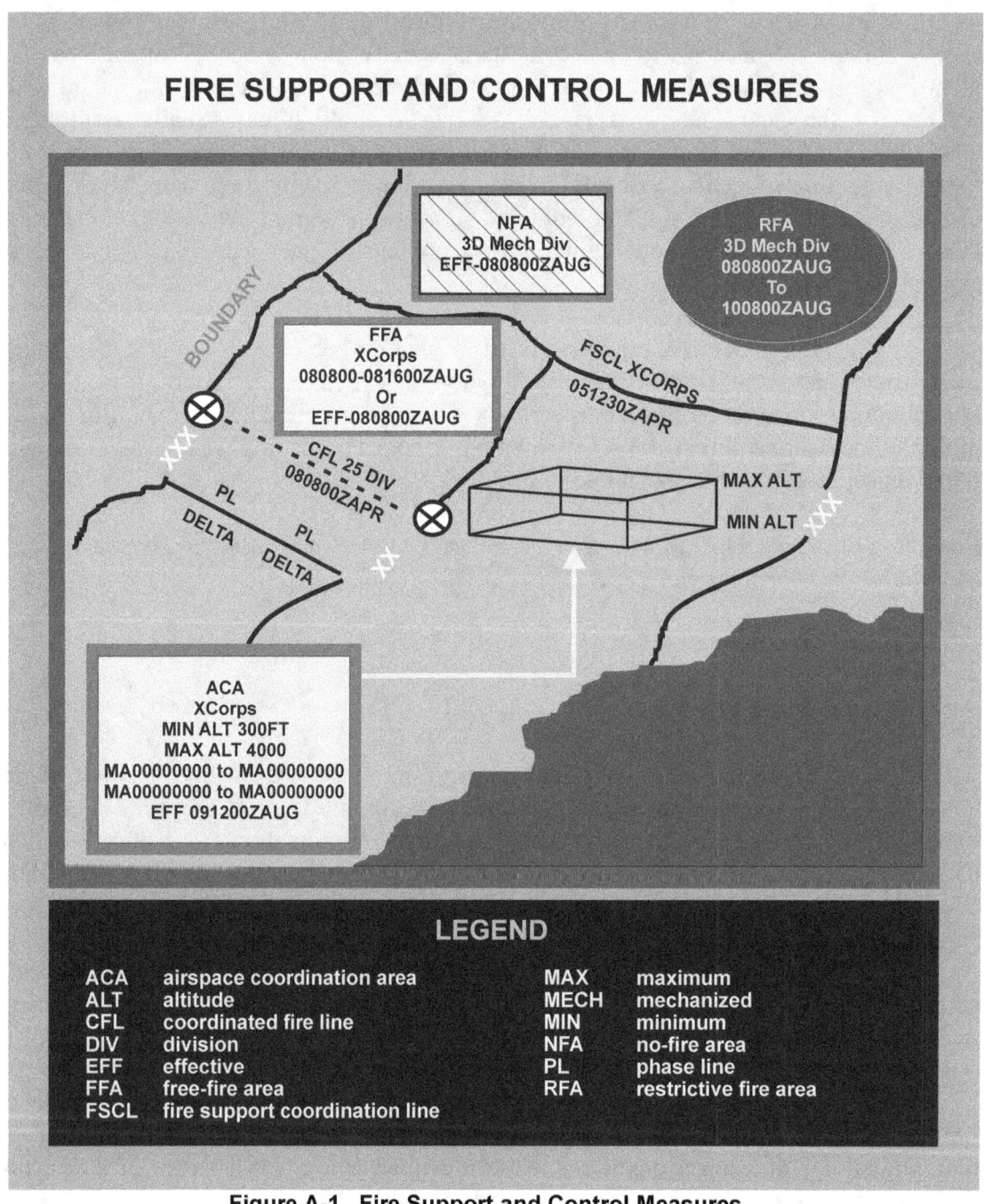

Figure A-1. Fire Support and Control Measures

FSCL applies to all fires of air, land, and sea-based weapon systems using any type of munition against surface targets (see Figure A-2).

(2) **Establishment.** An FSCL is established and adjusted by the appropriate land or amphibious force commanders within their boundaries in consultation with superior, subordinate, supporting, and affected commanders. The FSCL is a term oriented to air-land operations and is normally located only on land; however, in certain situations, such as littoral areas, the FSCL may affect both land and sea areas. If

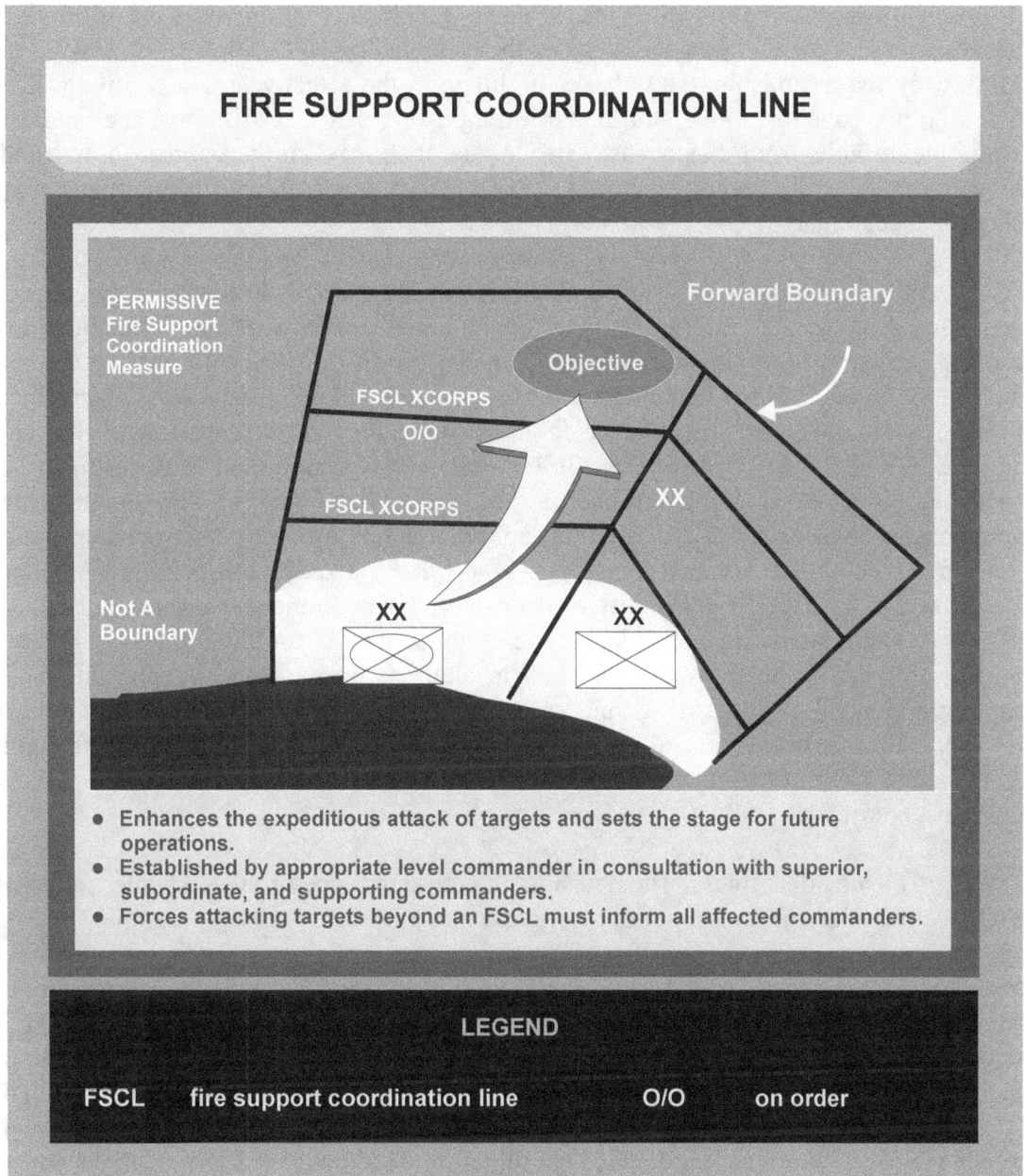

Figure A-2. Fire Support Coordination Line

possible, the FSCL should follow well-defined terrain features to assist identification from the air. In amphibious operations, the FSCL is normally established by the CLF after coordination with the CATF. Changes to the FSCL require notification of all affected forces within the AO and must allow sufficient time for these forces and/or components to incorporate the FSCL change. Current technology and collaboration tools between the elements of the joint force determine the times required for changing the FSCL. The JFC should establish a time standard in his guidance for shifting FSCLs. Whenever possible, restrictive measures are employed by commanders to enhance the protection of friendly forces operating beyond the FSCL — measures such as restrictive fire areas (RFAs) and no-fire areas (NFAs).

(3) **Graphic Portrayal.** The FSCL is graphically portrayed by a solid black line extending across the assigned areas of the establishing HQ. The letters "FSCL" are followed by the establishing HQ above the line and the effective DTG below the line. FSCLs do not have to follow "traditional" straight-line paths. Positioning the FSCL on terrain identifiable from the air is a technique that may further assist in fratricide prevention. Curved and/or enclosed FSCLs have applications in nonlinear joint operations (see Figure A-2).

(4) **Employment.** Use of an FSCL is not mandatory. Forces engaging targets beyond an FSCL must inform all affected commanders in sufficient time to allow necessary reaction to avoid fratricide, both in the air and on the land. In exceptional circumstances, the inability to conduct this coordination will not preclude the engagement of targets beyond the FSCL. However, failure to do so may increase the risk of fratricide and waste resources. Short of an FSCL, all air-to-ground and surface-to-surface engagement operations are controlled by the appropriate land or amphibious force commander. This control is exercised through the operations staff or with predesignated procedures. The FSCL is not a boundary — the synchronization of operations on either side of the FSCL is the responsibility of the establishing commander out to the limits of the land or amphibious force boundary. The establishment of an FSCL does not create a free-fire area (FFA) beyond the FSCL. When targets are engaged beyond an FSCL, supporting element's engagements must not produce adverse effects on or to the rear of the line. Engagements beyond the FSCL must be consistent with the establishing commander's priorities, timing, and desired effects and deconflicted whenever possible with the supported HQ.

(5) **Considerations.** The decision on where to place or even whether to use an FSCL requires careful consideration. If used, its location is based on estimates of the situation and CONOPS. Location of enemy forces, anticipated rates of movement, concept and tempo of the operation, organic weapon capabilities, and other factors are all considered by the commander. The FSCL is normally positioned closer to the FLOT in the defense than in the offense; however, the exact positioning depends on the situation. Placing the FSCL at greater depths will typically require support from higher organic HQ and other supporting commanders. Also, when the FSCL is positioned at greater depth, there is greater requirement for detailed coordination with the establishing commander.

(a) Air strikes short of the FSCL (both CAS and AI) must be under positive or procedural control to ensure proper clearance of joint fires (e.g., JTACs or FAC[A]s). Land commanders must consider the need for extra control measures.

(b) By establishing an FSCL close-in, yet at sufficient depth so as to not limit high-tempo maneuver, land and amphibious force commanders ease the coordination requirements for engagement operations within their AOs by forces not under their control such as NSFS or AI.

(c) Coordination of engagements beyond the FSCL is especially critical to commanders of air, land, and SOF units operating beyond the FSCL. Such coordination is also important when engaging forces are employing wide-area munitions or those with delayed effects. Finally, this coordination assists in avoiding conflicting or redundant engagement operations.

(d) The establishing commander adjusts the location of the FSCL as required to keep pace with operations. In high-tempo maneuver operations, the FSCL may change frequently. A series of predisseminated "on-order" FSCLs will help accelerate the coordination required. The establishing commander quickly transmits the change to higher, lower, adjacent, and supporting HQ to ensure engagement operations are appropriately coordinated by controlling agencies. Anticipated adjustments to the location of the FSCL are normally transmitted to other elements of the joint force sufficiently early to reduce potential disruptions in their current and near-term operations. Careful planning and coordination is essential for changes to the FSCL. This planning is necessary to minimize the risk of fratricide and avoid disrupting operations.

(e) Varying capabilities for acquisition and engagement may exist among adjacent commanders in a multinational operation. Normally, corps level commanders may establish an FSCL to support their operations. Layered FSCLs and multiple, separate, noncontiguous corps and/or MEF FSCLs positioned at varying depths create a coordination and execution challenge for supporting commanders (e.g., tracking effective times, lateral boundaries, and multiple command guidance). In cases such as these when the components share a mutual boundary, the JFC or JFLCC may consolidate the operational requirements of subordinates to establish a single FSCL. This FSCL may be noncontiguous, to reflect the varying capabilities of subordinate commands. A single FSCL facilitates air support, accommodates subordinate deep operations requirements, and eases coordination of FSCL changes.

c. **Free-Fire Area**

(1) **Purpose.** An FFA is a specific designated area into which any weapon system may fire without additional coordination with the establishing HQ. It is used to expedite joint fires and to facilitate jettison of aircraft munitions.

(2) **Establishment.** An FFA may be established only by the military commander with jurisdiction over the area (usually, a division or higher commander). Preferably, the FFA should be located on identifiable terrain; however, it may be designated by grid coordinates or GARS.

(3) **Graphic Portrayal.** The FFA is graphically portrayed by a solid black line defining the area and the letters "FFA" within, followed by the establishing HQ and the effective DTG (see Figure A-1).

d. **Kill Boxes**

(1) **Definition.** A kill box is a three-dimensional area used to facilitate the integration of joint fires.

(2) **Purpose.** When established, the primary purpose of a kill box is to allow lethal attack against surface targets without further coordination with the establishing commander and without terminal attack control. When used to integrate air-to-surface and surface-to-surface indirect fires, the kill box will have appropriate restrictions. The goal is to reduce the coordination required to fulfill support requirements with maximum flexibility, while preventing fratricide. A kill box will not be established specifically for CAS missions.

(3) **Establishment.** A kill box is established and adjusted by supported component commanders in consultation with superior, subordinate, supporting, and affected commanders, and is an extension of an existing support relationship established by the JFC.

See FM 3-09.34/MCRP 3-25H/NTTP 3-09.2.1/AFTTP(I) 3-2.59, Multi-Service Tactics, Techniques, and Procedures for Kill Box Employment, *for further information.*

3. **Restrictive Measures**

a. **Restrictive Fire Line**

(1) **Purpose.** The restrictive fire line (RFL) is a line established between converging friendly forces — one or both may be moving — that prohibits joint fires or the effects of joint fires across the line without coordination with the affected force. The purpose of the line is to prevent fratricide and duplication of engagements by converging friendly forces.

(2) **Establishment.** The commander common to the converging forces establishes the RFL. It is located on identifiable terrain when possible. In linkup operations, it is usually closer to the stationary force to allow maximum freedom of action for the maneuver and joint fire support of the linkup force.

(3) **Graphic Portrayal.** The RFL is graphically portrayed by a solid black line, with "RFL" followed by the establishing HQ above the line and the effective DTG below the line (see Figure A-3).

b. **No-Fire Area**

(1) **Purpose.** The purpose of the NFA is to prohibit joint fires or their effects into an area. There are two exceptions:

(a) When the establishing HQ approves joint fires within the NFA on a mission-by-mission basis.

(b) When an enemy force within the NFA engages a friendly force and the engaged commander determines there is a requirement for immediate protection and responds with the minimal force needed to defend the force.

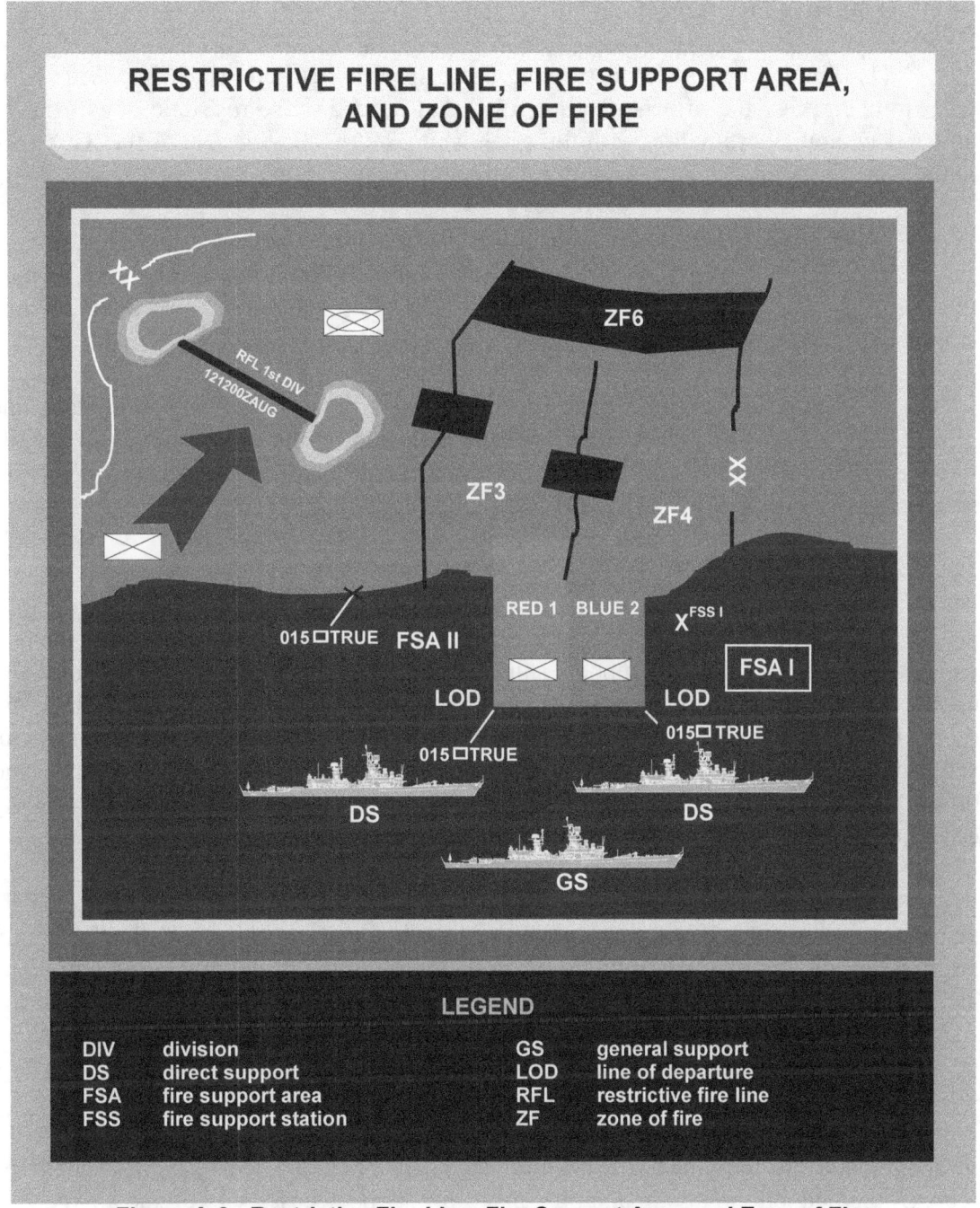

Figure A-3. Restrictive Fire Line, Fire Support Area, and Zone of Fire

(2) **Establishment.** Any size unit may establish NFAs. If possible, the NFA is established on identifiable terrain. It may also be located by a series of grids or by a radius from a center point.

(3) **Graphic Portrayal.** The NFA is graphically portrayed as an area outlined with a solid black line with black diagonal lines inside. The letters "NFA" are within, followed by the establishing HQ and the effective DTG (see Figure A-1).

c. **Restrictive Fire Area**

(1) **Purpose.** An RFA is an area where specific restrictions are imposed and in which joint fires, or the effects of joint fires, that exceed those restrictions will not be delivered without coordination with the establishing HQ. The purpose of the RFA is to regulate joint fires into an area according to the stated restrictions.

(2) **Establishment.** A maneuver battalion or higher echelon normally establishes an RFA. Usually, the RFA is located on identifiable terrain, by grid, or by a radius from a center point. To facilitate rapidly changing operations, on-call RFAs may be used. The dimensions, locations, and restrictions of the on-call RFA are prearranged.

(3) **Graphic Portrayal.** The RFA is graphically portrayed by a solid black line defining the area and the letters "RFA" within, followed by the establishing HQ and the effective DTG. The restrictions may be included within the graphic if space allows, or reference may be made to a specific OPORD or OPLAN (see Figure A-1).

d. **Zone of Fire**

(1) **Purpose.** A ZF is an FSCM that includes the area within which a designated ground unit or fire support ship delivers, or is prepared to deliver, joint fire support. Joint fires may or may not be observed. Land is divided into ZFs which are assigned to gunfire support ships and units as a means to coordinate their efforts with each other and with the scheme of maneuver of the supported ground unit. Units and ships assigned ZFs are responsible for engaging known targets and targets of opportunity according to their mission and the guidance of the supported commander.

(2) **Establishment.** The commander of the maritime force providing NSFS establishes and assigns ZFs for the forces. The ZF for an artillery battalion or a ship assigned the mission of DS normally corresponds to the AO of the supported unit. The ZF for an artillery battalion or a ship assigned the mission of GS should be within the boundaries of the supported unit. When used in conjunction with naval gunfire, the size and shape of a ZF will depend on the following:

(a) **Boundaries of Zone of Fire.** In order to permit ready identification by the spotter and the individual fire support ship, the boundaries of the ZFs should be recognizable both on the terrain and on a map. It may be necessary to divide a large ZFs into two or more smaller zones due to considerations discussed below. The boundaries of ZFs of DS ships should correspond to the zones of action of the LF units supported.

(b) **Size.** The size of each ZF should be such that the fire support ships, or ships assigned to observe and/or destroy targets, will be able to accomplish the mission in the time allocated. When ZFs are delineated, known or suspected targets scheduled for destruction in each zone are plotted, and then the number and type of targets are compared to the capability of the ship.

(c) **Visibility.** Observation from seaward is a desirable feature for ZFs, since it permits a ship to deliver more accurate and rapid fire.

(d) **Accessibility to Fire.** The ZFs must be accessible to the trajectory of the fire support ship(s) assigned to the zone.

(3) ZFs are also assigned to FA units by their higher HQ. The ZF for FA units assigned to a maneuver unit or assigned the mission of DS corresponds to the AO of the parent or supported maneuver unit. The ZF for an artillery unit assigned the mission of reinforcing corresponds to the ZF of the reinforced artillery unit. The ZF for an artillery unit assigned the mission of GS-reinforcing corresponds to the ZF of the reinforced artillery unit and is within the AO of the supported maneuver unit. The ZF for an artillery unit assigned the mission of GS corresponds to the AO of the supported maneuver unit.

(4) **Graphic Portrayal.** ZFs are delineated by the use of broken lines (solid lines if unit boundaries are used) and are designated by Arabic numerals, e.g., "ZF3" (see Figure A-3).

4. **Maneuver Control Measures**

a. **Boundaries**

(1) **Purpose.** A boundary is a maneuver control measure. In land warfare, it is a line by which surface AOs between adjacent units and/or formations are defined. Boundaries designate the geographical limits of the AO of a unit. Within their own boundaries, units may execute joint fires and maneuver without close coordination with neighboring units unless otherwise restricted. Normally, units do not fire across boundaries unless the fires are coordinated with the adjacent unit or the fires are beyond an FSCM, such as a CFL. These restrictions apply to conventional and special munitions and their effects. When fires such as smoke and illumination affect an adjacent unit, coordination with that unit is normally required. A commander can, in certain situations, decide to fire across boundaries at positively identified enemy elements without coordination. However, direct and observed joint fires should be used when firing across boundaries at positively identified enemy forces when there is no time to coordinate with adjacent friendly units.

(2) **Establishment and/or Portrayal.** Any commander given an AO can establish boundaries for subordinate units. These boundaries will be respected by all Service and functional components. Boundaries are depicted as solid black lines with a symbol placed on the boundary to show the size and designation of the highest echelons that have the boundary in common. If the units are of unequal size, the symbol of the higher unit is shown and the designation of the lower unit is given completely (see Figure A-1).

Control and Coordination Measures

b. **Phase Lines**

(1) **Purpose.** A phase line (PL) is a maneuver control measure used by land forces for control and coordination of military operations. It is usually a recognizable terrain feature extending across the zone of action. Units normally report crossing PLs, but do not halt unless specifically directed. PLs can be used to identify limits of advance, monitor rates of movement, control joint fires (when dual designated as an FSCM), or define an AO. The purpose of each PL and any actions required by forces affected by the PL will be specified on the OPORD of the establishing HQ.

(2) **Establishment and/or Portrayal.** Any commander given an AO can establish PLs. A PL is depicted as a solid black line labeled "PL" and assigned letters, numbers, or code name designations (see Figure A-1).

c. **Fire Support Area and/or Fire Support Station**

(1) **Purpose.** A fire support area (FSA) is an appropriate maneuver area assigned to fire support ships by the maritime commander from which they deliver surface joint fire support to an operation ashore. An FSA is normally associated with amphibious operations but can be used whenever it is desirable to have a fire support ship occupy a certain geographic position. A fire support station (FSS) is an exact location at sea from which a fire support ship delivers fires. This designation is used to station ships in order to be able to reach certain targets. For example, a ship in an FSA may not be able to reach a certain target except when it is stationed at the FSS.

(2) **Establishment.** The officer in tactical command, typically the CATF, establishes FSAs and FSSs. In amphibious operations when engagement groups are formed and separate landing areas are designated, the CATF may assign each engagement group commander the responsibility for control of naval gunfire support within the area.

(3) **Graphic Portrayal.** FSAs are designed with Roman numerals (FSA I, II, III) and are shown on the NSFS operations overlay. FSSs are designated by numbers (FSS 1, 2, 3) and are shown on the NSFS operations overlay as an X indicating the exact position of the ship (see Figure A-3).

5. **Airspace Coordinating Measures**

a. **Airspace Coordinating Measures.** ACMs are critical to the successful employment of joint fires. A key to effectively coordinating joint fires is to constantly view the operational environment as a three dimensional area. ACMs are nominated from subordinate HQ through component command HQ, and forwarded to the airspace control authority in accordance with the air control plan. Most ACMs impact on direct and indirect joint fires trajectories and UASs because of their airspace use. Some ACMs may be established to permit surface joint fires or UAS operations. The component commanders ensure that ACM nominations support and do not conflict with joint operations prior to forwarding to the JAOC. The airspace control authority approves formal ACM nominations and includes them in the ACO. The airspace control authority consolidates, coordinates, and deconflicts the airspace requirements of the components and publishes the ACMs in the ACO. The ACO is normally published at least daily and is often distributed both separately and as a section of the ATO.

See JP 3-52, Joint Airspace Control, *and JP 3-30,* Command and Control for Joint Air Operations, *for further information on C2 of air operations.*

b. Normally, ACMs such as minimum risk routes will terminate in the vicinity of the FSCL. However, the situation may require establishing active and planned ACMs beyond the FSCL to facilitate rapid change of both the FSCL and ACM. ACMs may be established to facilitate operations between the FSCL and the land force commander's forward boundary. Ground infiltration and aerial insertion and/or extraction of SOF or long-range surveillance teams as well as attack helicopter maneuver are operational examples.

c. Changes to ACMs within a land force AO are initiated by the component's air control element with airspace control authority approval. One common procedural ACM that impacts on the delivery of aerial fire support is a coordinating altitude. A coordinating altitude separates fixed- and rotary-wing aircraft. The JFC approves the coordinating altitude, which is normally specified in the air control plan. The airspace control authority is the final approving authority for changes, which are requested through airspace coordination channels. Fixed- or rotary-wing aircraft planning extended operations penetrating this altitude should, whenever possible, notify the appropriate airspace control facility.

d. **Airspace Coordination Area (ACA).** The ACA is the primary ACM which reflects the coordination of airspace for use by air support and indirect joint fires.

(1) **Purpose.** ACAs are used to ensure aircrew safety and the effective use of indirect supporting surface joint fires by deconfliction through time and space. The ACA is a block or corridor of airspace in which friendly aircraft are reasonably safe from friendly surface fires. A formal ACA (a three dimensional box of airspace) requires detailed planning. More often an informal ACA is established using time, lateral separation, or altitude to provide separation between surface-to-surface and air-delivered weapon effects.

For additional information on the ACA, see JP 3-09.3, Close Air Support, *and JP 3-52,* Joint Airspace Control.

(2) **Establishment.** The airspace control authority establishes formal ACAs at the request of the appropriate component commander. ACAs require detailed planning. Though not always necessary, formal ACAs should be considered. Vital information defining the formal ACA includes minimum and maximum altitudes, a baseline designated by grid coordinates at each end, the width (on either side of the baseline), and

the effective times. When time for coordination is limited, an informal ACA is used. In an informal ACA, aircraft and surface joint fires may be separated by time or distance (lateral, altitude, or a combination of the two). The informal ACA can be requested by the maneuver commander requesting CAS or employing helicopters, and is approved at battalion or higher level. Both types of ACAs are constructed with the assistance of the air liaison officer to ensure they meet the technical requirements of the aircraft and weapon systems.

(3) **Graphic Portrayal.** A formal ACA is shown as an area enclosed by a solid black line. Depicted inside the enclosed area are "ACA," the establishing HQ, the minimum and maximum altitudes, the grid coordinates for each end of the baseline, and the effective DTG or the words "on order." Informal ACAs are not normally displayed on maps, charts, or overlays (see Figure A-1).

Intentionally Blank

APPENDIX B
JOINT FIRE SUPPORT OPERATION ORDER FORMAT

ANNEX XX (JOINT FIRE SUPPORT) TO OPERATION ORDER NO## [code name] — [issuing HQ]

(Include heading if annex distributed separately from OPLAN/OPORD.)

1. **SITUATION**

    a. Enemy Forces

        (1) Include a detailed description of enemy fire support and air defense assets.

        (2) List enemy rocket, cannon, missile, and air force units. Include those organic to maneuver units. List all fire support units that can be identified as being committed or reinforcing. Consider all identified fire support units within supporting range as being in support of the committed force. Include the number of possible enemy air sorties by day, if known. Estimate the number, type, yield, and delivery means of enemy chemical, biological, radiological, and nuclear weapons available to the committed force.

    b. Friendly Forces

        (1) State the concept of fires.

        (2) Provide adjacent units' concept of fires, if applicable.

        (3) Include supporting air, land, and maritime forces.

    c. Environment

        (1) **Terrain.** List terrain aspects that would impact operations.

        (2) **Weather.** List weather aspects that would impact operations.

        (3) **Civil considerations.** List civil considerations that would impact operations. Refer to civil-military operations annex as required.

2. **MISSION.** State the joint fire support mission for the operation.

3. **EXECUTION**

    a. **Concept of Joint Fires.** Describe how joint fires will be used to support the CONOPS. State the priority of joint fire support. This must be consistent with what is in the concept of fires in the OPORD/OPLAN. Address the objectives for using air, land, and maritime fires.

b. **Air Component**

(1) **General.** Briefly describe the air commander's concept for the use of air power.

(2) **Air interdiction.**

(3) **Close air support.**

(4) **Electronic attack.** Refer to IO annex as required.

(5) **Intelligence, reconnaissance, and surveillance operations.** Refer to ISR annex as required.

(6) **Miscellaneous.** State the following:

(a) The ATO's effective time period.

(b) Deadlines for submission of AI, CAS, search and rescue, and EW requests.

(c) The mission request numbering system based on the target numbering system.

(d) Joint suppression of enemy air defense taskings from the land component commander.

(e) Essential ACA measures — such as coordinating altitude, target areas, minimum risk route requirements — identified in the ACA annex.

c. **Land Component**

(1) **General.** Include the concept for use of cannon, mortar, rocket, and missile fires in support of shaping operations.

(2) **Organization for combat.**

(3) **Allocation of ammunition.**

(4) **Miscellaneous.** Include the following:

(a) Changes to the targeting numbering system.

(b) The use of pulse repetition frequency (PRF) codes.

(c) Positioning restrictions.

d. **Maritime Component**

(1) **General.** Include the concept for use of NSFS and TLAMs.

(2) **NSFS Organization.**

(3) **Miscellaneous.**

(a) Trajectory limitations or minimum safe distances.

(b) Frequency allocations.

(c) Reference to an NSFS annex.

e. **Nuclear Operations**

f. **Smoke Operations**

g. **Target Acquisition.** Include information pertaining to the employment and allocation of TA systems and EW assets.

h. **Coordinating Instructions**

(1) List the targeting products (target selection standards matrix, HPT list, and attack guidance matrix).

(2) List FSCMs.

(3) Refer to time of execution of program of fires.

(4) Include ROE.

(5) List fire support rehearsal times and requirements.

(6) List target allocations.

(7) Specify the datum or coordinate system to be used.

4. **SERVICE SUPPORT.** Identify the location of munition transfer points and ammunition supply points, or refer to the logistics annex. List the controlled supply rate.

5. **COMMAND AND SIGNAL**

APPENDIXES:

1. Air Component Support

2. Land Component Support

3. Maritime Component Support

4. SO Component

DISTRIBUTION: (If distributed separately from OPLAN/OPORD)

APPENDIX C
LASER-GUIDED SYSTEMS

1. General

a. Laser-guided systems provide the joint force with the ability to locate and engage targets with an increased first-round hit probability. Laser-guided systems can effectively engage a wide range of targets, including moving targets. Laser-guided weapons (LGWs) can reduce the number of weapons and/or weapon systems required to create an effect or achieve an objective, because of increased accuracy. Based on the threat level and environment, laser-guided systems provide additional capabilities, but also have distinct limitations. In any laser designating situation, strive for simplicity and use all available resources to help ensure first-pass success.

b. **Laser Capabilities.** Laser designators radiate a narrow beam of pulsed energy. Current tactical lasers operate in the near infrared wavelength spectrum, which is not visible to the human eye. When within range, the laser designator can be aimed so the energy precisely designates a chosen spot on the target. Laser target designators (LTDs) mark targets for laser spot trackers (LSTs) and LGWs. Some laser systems can accurately determine target range and location. When coupled with horizontal and vertical scales, they can measure target azimuth and elevation.

c. **Laser Target Ranging and Designation Systems.** Laser target ranging and designation systems can provide accurate range, azimuth, and elevation information to locate enemy targets. These systems may vary from handheld to aircraft-mounted devices and perform similar functions with varying degrees of accuracy. In combination with GPS, lasers can provide accurate enemy target locations. In addition, lasers in combination with GPS can provide for target area analysis. This analysis can be used to fire weapons accurately at the enemy, to accurately locate future friendly observer locations, and to enable friendly forces to effectively conduct maneuver operations as well as command and control their forces by accurate identification of terrain reference points.

d. **Laser Acquisition Devices.** Of the **two types** of laser acquisition devices, **the first, the LST, is used to aid visual acquisition of the target** to be attacked by another weapon. This type of laser acquisition device is normally mounted on fixed-wing aircraft or helicopters. **The second type of acquisition device is a seeker and guidance kit** mounted on LGWs which guide on coded laser energy.

e. **Basic Considerations.** There are five basic considerations for using LSTs or LGWs:

(1) **Line of sight (LOS)** must exist between the designator and the target and between the target and the LST/LGW.

(2) **PRF codes** of the laser designator and the LST/LGW must be compatible.

(3) **The direction of attack** must allow the LST/LGW to sense enough reflected laser energy from the target for the seeker to acquire and lock on the target.

(4) **The LTD** must designate the target at the correct time, and for the correct length of time. If the length of time is insufficient, the seeker head could break lock and the flight pattern of the LGW becomes unpredictable.

(5) **The delivery system (air or ground)** must deliver the LGW within the specific LGW envelope to ensure the weapon can physically reach the target. There is an **increased hazard to friendly forces** when aircrews release weapons behind friendly lines.

f. **Environmental factors can affect laser designators and seeker head performance.** Tactics and techniques must consider low clouds and fog, smoke, haze, snow and rain, solar saturation, and other visually limiting phenomena.

g. **Beam divergence and target size.** Laser spot size is a function of beam divergence and the distance from the laser designator to the target. If an LTD has a beam spread or divergence of 1 milliradian, its spot would have a diameter of approximately one meter at a distance of 1,000 meters in front of the designator. If this spot were aimed at a 3-meter by 3-meter box 3,000 meters away the laser spot would be as wide and tall as the box.

h. **Target Reflection.** Most surfaces have a mixture of mirror-like and scattered reflections. Laser energy reflects in an arc, but is strongest at the angle where it would reflect if the surface were a mirror. If the LTD is perpendicular to a surface the reflection can be seen from all angles on the designated side, but can be detected best near the laser to target line (LTL), which is a line from the LTD to the target usually expressed in degrees magnetic. When the surface is at an angle to the laser designator, the angle of strongest reflection is also predictable. Glass, water, and highly polished surfaces are poor surfaces to designate because they reflect laser energy in only one direction. This requires the seeker to be in this small region and looking toward the reflected energy to achieve TA. Battlefield dynamics will rarely provide the opportunity to perfectly align laser designation/reflectivity in the direction of approaching aircraft or munitions. Strict adherence to laser cones or baskets and center mass target designation will best ensure success.

i. **Opponent Use of Laser Countermeasures.** US opponents realize the **importance of laser countermeasures** in a conflict with the United States or its multinational partners. Many of the techniques for countering laser energy and sensitive electro-optical equipment are common knowledge throughout much of the world. US opponents are well-equipped to detect and counter the sophisticated laser designator and guidance systems used by the armed forces of Western nations.

j. **Legal Uses of Lasers on the Battlefield.** Protocol IV to the Certain Conventional Weapons Convention (Protocol on Blinding Laser Weapons) **prohibits the use of lasers**

specifically designed to cause permanent blindness to unenhanced vision. For all other types of lasers, such as those used for detection, targeting, range-finding, communications, and target destruction, parties to the Protocol have an obligation to **"take all feasible precautions to avoid the incidence of permanent blindness to unenhanced vision."** The DOD Policy on Blinding Lasers recognizes that accidental or incidental eye injuries may occur on the battlefield through the use of lasers for detection, targeting, range-finding, communications, and target destruction; however, it is DOD policy "to strive, through training and doctrine, to minimize these injuries."

For a discussion of laser-guided considerations for CAS, see JP 3-09.3, Close Air Support.

For additional information on laser operations, see FM 3-09.32/MCRP 3-16.6A/NTTP 3-09.2/AFTTP(I) 3-2.6, JFIRE, Multi-Service Tactics, Techniques, and Procedures for the Joint Application of Firepower.

2.   **Laser Hardware**

a. **Laser-Guided Weapons.** All LGWs home on PRF-coded reflected laser energy. Some LGWs require target lock-on before launch (LOBL) and during the entire time of flight. Other LGWs allow target lock-on after launch (LOAL) and require illumination only during the terminal portion of flight. All LGWs require illumination until weapon impact. Typical laser-guided weapons include:

(1) **Laser-guided bombs (LGBs).** Paveway II, III, and enhanced Paveway III (GPS aided).

(2) **Laser-guided missiles (LGMs).** AGM-65E Laser Maverick and AGM-114 HELLFIRE. **LGMs generally provide greater standoff launch ranges than LGBs.** Greater range provides increased survivability for aircrews operating in a high threat environment. Aircrews and JTACs must exercise caution when launching LGMs from behind friendly troops.

(a) Laser Maverick employment considerations include:

1. In the event the laser signal is lost, the weapon will safe itself and overfly the target. The Maverick system allows aircrew to engage targets designated by either air or ground sources with inflight selectable PRF codes.

2. Delivery aircraft must have unobstructed LOS to the target to achieve Maverick lock-on.

3. The missile requires LOBL.

4. The Maverick and the laser designator must be set to the same PRF code prior to launch.

<u>5.</u> For other than self-designation, the attack heading must be adjusted to optimize the reflected laser energy.

(b) Hellfire employment considerations include:

<u>1.</u> In the event the laser signal is lost after lock-on, the missile seeker is programmed to begin searching for properly coded laser energy. The Hellfire system allows aircrews to engage targets designated by either air (buddy or autonomous, fixed wing or rotary wing) or ground forces with inflight selectable PRF codes.

<u>2.</u> The Hellfire can be employed in a LOBL or LOAL mode. In LOBL, the missile must acquire the laser energy prior to launch. In LOAL, the missile can be fired from defilade or behind a mask and climbs on a preprogrammed profile, searching for properly coded laser energy as it executes its fly-out. The trajectory of the missile can be altered by delaying laser designation.

<u>3.</u> The Hellfire missile uses last pulse logic in case of under spill and to protect the designator. The missile will hit the most distant laser spot within the seeker field of view.

<u>4.</u> The Hellfire is unimpeded by ceilings of 2,000 feet (ft) above ground level (AGL) and above. For employment under ceilings below 2,000 ft the aircrew will vary the missile mode, designator delay, and employment range to shape the trajectory. The rule of thumb minimum ceiling for Hellfire employment is 500 ft AGL.

(3) **Cannon Launched Guided Projectile - Copperhead**

(a) Copperhead is a 155-millimeter, cannon-launched, guided projectile with a shaped-charge warhead and a laser seeker. When fired at a moving or stationary hard point target, Copperhead homes in on laser energy reflected from the target during the final part of its trajectory. A remote laser designator provides laser energy. Copperhead is best used against multiple targets in large target arrays outside the range of maneuver direct fire weapon systems (approximately 3,000 meters). Copperhead may engage a single target or very few widely separated targets if they are HPTs; for example, an enemy commander's vehicle. Targets appearing within the range of maneuver direct fire weapon systems should be engaged by Copperhead only when the maneuver commander directs or when the direct fire systems are unable to engage the targets.

(b) Copperhead targets can be engaged as either planned targets or targets of opportunity. Planned targets are preferred because the firing battery requires less reaction time. Most often, the target-of-opportunity technique is used only during offensive operations.

For more information on Copperhead employment, see FM 3-09.42, Fire Support for the Brigade Combat Team.

(4) **Laser-Equipped UASs**

(a) **General Procedures**

<u>1.</u> **Employment.** Laser-equipped UASs utilize the same procedures and communications as an airborne laser designator operator (LDO). In some cases, the UAS may also act as a strike aircraft, using the same procedures as other strike aircraft.

<u>2.</u> **Target Acquisition Considerations.** If a laser-equipped UAS is being utilized by the LDO, coordination between the UAS flight crew and the attack aircrew is critical for both safety and laser geometry. LST-equipped strike aircraft should notify the LDO that they are LST capable upon arriving on-station. The LDO, through standard communication, will then direct the UAS mark onto the target. The LDO may pass the UAS laser PRF code to the attack aircraft, or the attack aircraft may pass its weapons code to the LDO.

<u>3.</u> **Deconfliction of Airspace.** Standard procedures used by LDOs to deconflict fixed-wing and rotary-wing aircraft apply to laser-equipped UASs employed on laser designation operations. Proper laser geometry and 2,000-ft altitude blocks for the UAS stationing orbit are recommended when using a UAS to mark for strike aircraft.

b. **Laser Target Designators.** Ground laser target designators (GLTDs) are employed by ground forces to illuminate targets with laser energy. LGWs use this energy to guide to the target. LSTs use the reflected laser energy as a reference point for lock-on and tracking. The laser energy PRF is adjustable and must match the PRF setting on the weapon or tracker. GLTD ranges vary from 10 meters to 5 kilometers. Airborne laser target designators (ALTDs) are carried on aircraft and provide the same function as the GLTD. ALTDs are capable of very long range lasing and are normally employed below 30,000 ft AGL. See Figure C-1 for advantages and disadvantages of airborne and ground designators.

Note: The PRF of LGBs is normally only adjustable prior to flight and cannot be changed once airborne. Most missiles such as Maverick and Hellfire can be adjusted in-flight. JTACs and aircrews must ensure the laser designator PRF matches the code programmed into the weapon or the weapon will not guide.

c. **Laser Rangefinders/Target Locating Devices.** Laser rangefinders (LRFs) use low power laser pulses to measure range to an object. **Digital magnetic compass systems will not provide the accuracy needed for a single inertially-aided munition weapon to hit a point target.** Target locating devices are devices that incorporate an LRF, magnetic or gyroscopic compass, tilt measurement devices, and GPS. These systems measure the range and angles from its position provided by the GPS to mathematically derive a target location. If used correctly the quality of the target location is generally much better than that of a hand-derived coordinate. The accuracy of the coordinate is dependent on many variables. **Errors are induced by inaccurate GPS data, poor azimuth, range and elevation data, system calibration, and user skill.**

AIRBORNE AND GROUND DESIGNATOR ADVANTAGES AND DISADVANTAGES

TYPE DESIGNATORS	ADVANTAGES	DISADVANTAGES
AIRBORNE	Increased standoff Larger target area footprint	Larger laser spot size Increased susceptibility to podium effect
1. Trail Position	Increased probability of success (spot detection) Increased standoff	Axis restrictive Increased platform predictability
2. Overhead Wheel Position	Decreased platform predictability Good standoff	Decreased effectiveness in target areas with varying vertical developments (podium effect)
3. Offset or Opposing Wheel Position	Decreased platform predictability Excellent standoff	Axis restrictive Increased susceptibility to podium effect Coordination intensive
GROUND	Smaller laser spot size Decreased targeting ambiguity Rapid battle damage assessment	Axis restrictive Increased designator exposure Coordination intensive

Figure C-1. Airborne and Ground Designator Advantages and Disadvantages

These errors are magnified with range and can result in significant TLEs. Due to the variables listed previously, TLEs may vary from 10 meters at 1 kilometer to more than 300 meters at maximum ranges.

d. **Laser Spot Trackers.** LSTs are systems that allow acquisition of a coded laser designated target. LSTs are laser sensors that provide heads up display cueing for aircraft equipped with these systems. While scanning for laser energy, these systems have a limited field of view that depends on range and switch settings. In general, the chances of acquisition are improved when cueing aids such as target marks, landmarks, and inertial navigation system/GPS coordinates help the pilot point the aircraft in the direction of the target.

3. **Laser Designation Operations**

a. **Laser designation operations** are divided into three primary categories: laser target ranging, TA, and weapons guidance.

(1) **Target Ranging.** Target ranging systems can provide accurate range, azimuth, and elevation information to identified targets.

(2) **Target Acquisition.** TA involves the use of an LST carried by the aircraft and an LTD aimed by a ground team or in some cases from the same or another aircraft.

(3) **Weapons Guidance.** Weapons guidance allows an LGW to home in on reflected laser energy placed on a target by an LTD. This allows precision delivery of weapons, some at standoff distances.

b. **Laser Designation Position.** In selecting a laser designation position, the LDO must consider LOS, expected munitions trajectory, tactical situation, cover and concealment, weather, and communications requirements. **The LDO should select positions that are near expected locations of high priority targets while minimizing risks to friendly forces.** If redundant LTDs are going to be employed, mutual support and coordination with maneuver elements should be addressed. The observer or controller team should determine its position as accurately as possible.

c. **Employment.** When employing LSTs, GLTDs, and LGWs, the following procedures will be used.

(1) **Attack headings** and LTLs, sometimes called designator target lines or pointer target lines, are normally pre-coordinated between the LDO and LGW-employing aircrew. The LTL is normally expressed in degrees magnetic unless otherwise requested.

(2) **Safety Zone.** Due to the possibility of false target indications from atmospheric scatter of the laser beam close to the laser exit port, attack headings should avoid the safety zone unless the tactical situation safely dictates otherwise. **The safety zone** is defined as a volume of airspace in the shape of a cone (generally 20 degrees) whose apex is at the target and extends equidistant either side of the target-to-laser designator line (see Figure C-2). This cone has a limit of plus or minus 10 degrees in the horizontal plane and a vertical limit of 20 degrees. Aircraft may engage targets from above the cone, as long as they remain above the 20 degrees. This safety zone will primarily affect low altitude delivery aircraft passing close to the LDO location. The minimum safe altitude for aircraft will vary with the aircraft's distance from the target. Aircrews may have difficulty determining how high they need to fly to remain above the 20-degree cone. Due to the possibility of false target indications, final attack headings must avoid the 20-degree safety exclusion zone, unless the tactical situation dictates otherwise.

(3) **Fratricide. Designator profiles behind the launch platform are inherently the safest and will minimize the possibility of fratricide. The possibility of fratricide still exists while operating anywhere within the optimal attack zone.** It is highest in the designated safety zone or when a false lock-on is achieved. Attack headings should be planned with consideration for friendly forces and noncombatant civilian locations. Ultimately the primary mechanisms for limiting fratricide are command emphasis, disciplined operations, close coordination among component commands, rehearsals, and enhanced SA.

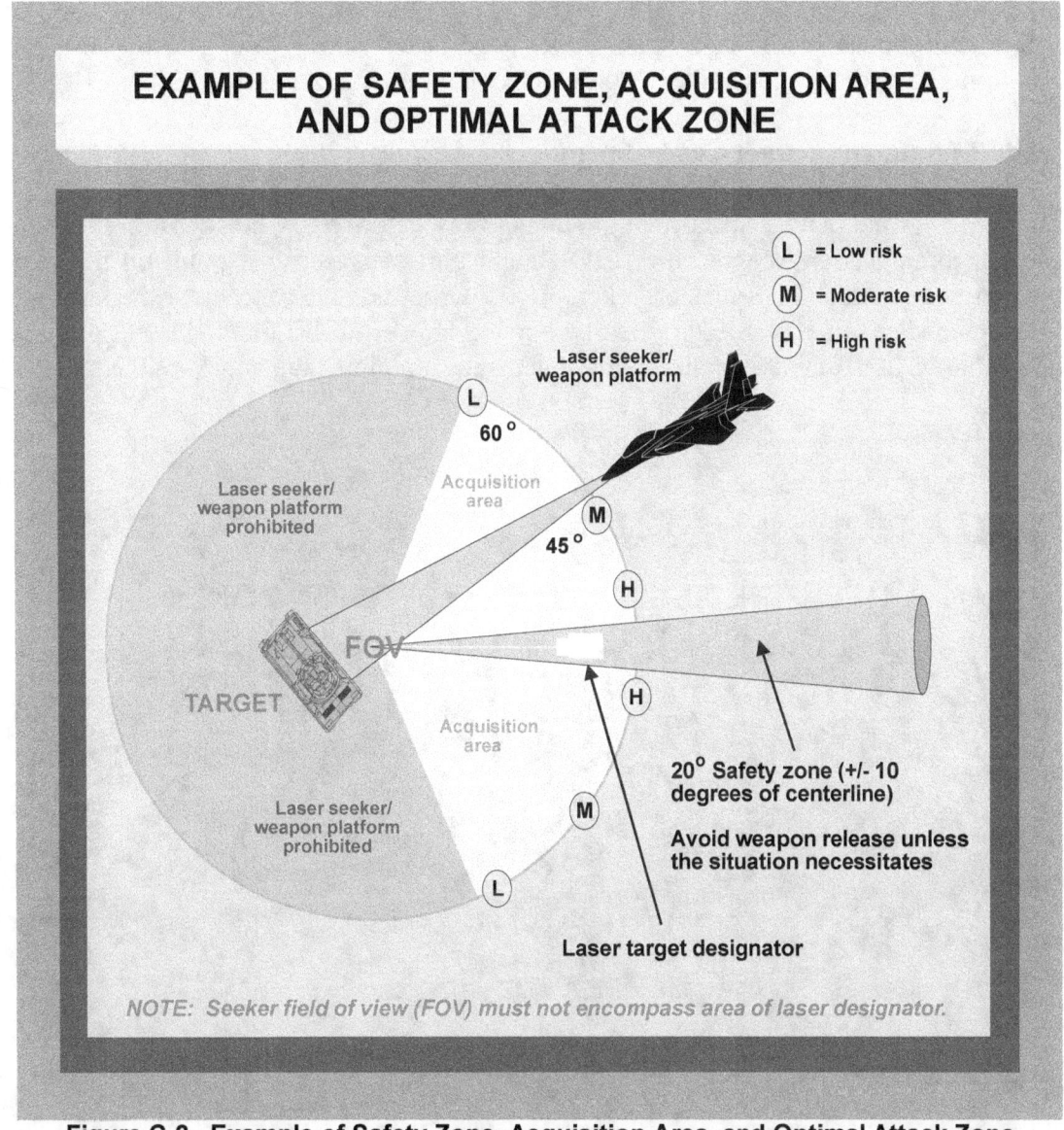

EXAMPLE OF SAFETY ZONE, ACQUISITION AREA, AND OPTIMAL ATTACK ZONE

L = Low risk

M = Moderate risk

H = High risk

Laser seeker/weapon platform

Laser seeker/weapon platform prohibited

Acquisition area

60°

45°

FOV

TARGET

Acquisition area

Laser seeker/weapon platform prohibited

20° Safety zone (+/- 10 degrees of centerline)

Avoid weapon release unless the situation necessitates

Laser target designator

NOTE: Seeker field of view (FOV) must not encompass area of laser designator.

Figure C-2. Example of Safety Zone, Acquisition Area, and Optimal Attack Zone

(4) The **attack zone** is inside a 120-degree cone whose apex is at the target and extends to 60 degrees on either side of the target-to-laser designator line and is outside the 20-degree safety zone. To give the laser trackers/weapons a better chance of acquiring the reflected laser spot, a smaller, 90-degree, cone (+/–45 degrees) is preferred, and the optimum attack axis is normally from 10 to 45 degrees on either side of the target-to-laser designator line.

(5) Aircrews should verify that they are attacking the correct target through additional means (such as visual description, terrain features, and non-laser target marks).

(6) **Hellfire Designator Exclusion Zone.** The LTL must be given to the aircrew in degrees magnetic. The aircrew needs this information to align the helicopter, ensuring positive seeker lock-on of the LGM for LOBL delivery or positive in-flight

seeker lock-on of the LGM for LOAL. The LTL will also allow the aircrew to prevent inadvertently engaging the LTD. The LDO must be outside a 30-degree by 40-degree zone from the aircraft, but within a 120-degree cone from the target (see Figure C-3).

d. **Terrain and Target Concealment**

(1) If the LDO suspects that the **target may be partially masked** from the view of the incoming laser weapon, the LDO should aim the laser at a point on the target believed to be within LOS of the seeker. If the target is well concealed, the laser spot may be aimed at some overhead or nearby object. However, this method is not preferred and should be used only when the situation demands an immediate attack on the target.

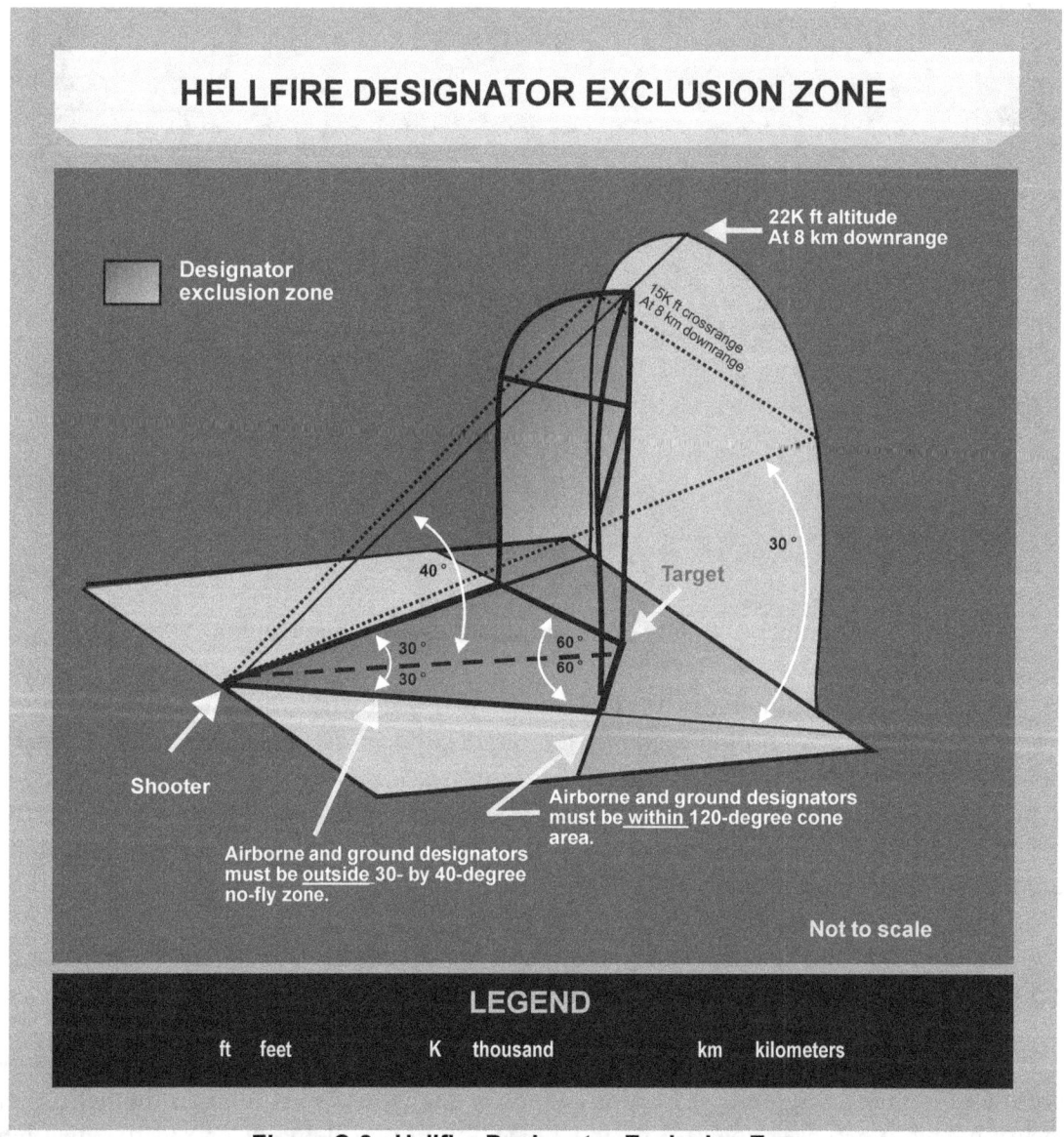

Figure C-3. Hellfire Designator Exclusion Zone

(2) If a designated mobile **target moves out of the view** of the LDO, it may still be possible to salvage the attack. A point near the target may be designated until the target again comes into view or until designation responsibility can be passed to another operator who has the target in sight. It is also possible to move the laser spot to another target in the immediate vicinity. If the LST or LGW has already locked on, the laser spot should be moved slowly and without interrupting laser output to the new target location.

e. **LDO Survivability.** To enhance survivability, the LDO should keep designation time to the minimum necessary for the weapon or seeker being used. This reduces the time available for the enemy to detect, locate, and act to suppress the LTD and/or LDO.

f. **Laser Designation Timing.** Successful use of LGWs or LSTs depends on the ability of the LDO to designate the target at the proper time. Laser designation must be closely coordinated with the delivery of an LGW. Timing requirements should take into account the following:

(1) Weapons **requiring** LOBL.

(2) Weapons allowing LOAL.

(3) Remaining LTD battery life (if applicable).

(4) Laser radiation time constraints due to overheating.

(5) Susceptibility to laser countermeasures.

g. **Joint Interoperability.** Laser designation operations and weapons delivery units must have compatible and secure communications equipment and common secure codes or the authentication codes necessary for joint communications on non-secure nets.

4. **Execution Considerations**

a. **Target Acquisition Considerations**

(1) Using LTDs can provide a fast and accurate means of marking targets for both LGWs and LST-equipped aircraft. Using target coordinates, smoke, and illuminating flares complements LTD target-marking and improves the chances for successful first pass TA. Without cueing, aircraft may be pointed too far away from the target to acquire the laser spot. Therefore, when the tactical situation allows, supplemental marking is recommended to avoid losing sorties or having to re-attack. Care should be taken to avoid obscuring the target with the visual mark.

(2) **Attack Angles.** Aircrews release or launch LGWs so the reflected laser energy will be within the seeker field of view at the appropriate time. The maximum allowable attack angle (laser-to-target/seeker-to-target) depends upon the characteristics

of the weapon system employed. If the angle is too large, the seeker will not receive enough reflected energy to sense the laser spot.

(3) **Coordination with JTAC.** If the attack aircraft has an LST, the JTAC can designate the target for aircrew identification. The aircrew can use the LST to visually locate the target. Once the aircrew locates the target, it can conduct an attack using unguided ordnance.

(4) **Employment of LGBs in conjunction with coded LTDs is either autonomous or assisted.** Autonomous LGB employment uses the CAS aircraft's onboard LTD for terminal weapons guidance. Most aircraft capable of delivering LGBs can provide on-board autonomous self-designation. Assisted LGB employment uses an off-board LTD for terminal weapons guidance. This is typically accomplished by a ground team operating a GLTD (such as a ground/vehicle laser locator designator) or by another aircraft (known as buddy lasing). Aircraft without on-board ALTDs that can carry and deliver LGBs but have no on-board terminal weapons guidance capability require assisted LGB employment. **Coded LTDs are ground and airborne systems that have two specific purposes.** First, they provide terminal weapons guidance for LGWs. Second, they designate targets for coded LSTs. Coded LTDs emit laser energy with a PRF and require input of specific laser codes for operation. Codes are assigned to LGWs and directly relate to the PRF that harmonizes the designator and seeker interface. **Coded LTDs used for terminal weapons guidance must be set to the same code as the LGW.** Certain LGWs, such as LGBs, are coded prior to takeoff and cannot be changed once the aircraft is airborne. However, all coded LTDs, with the exception of the AC-130H, can change codes while airborne. (Note: The AC-130H's LTD is permanently preset with only one code [1688] and cannot be changed.) The JTAC will have to coordinate efforts to ensure both the aircraft and designator are on the same code. Coordination for the LTD to match the LGW code is conducted through the ATO, DASC/ASOC, or JTAC nine-line briefing. Sometimes, an LTD will serve the dual purpose of target designation for a coded laser acquisition/spot tracker and terminal weapons guidance for LGWs. In these cases, the LTD, LST, and LGW must have the same code. Laser codes are always passed as four digits to avoid confusion. When briefing LST-equipped aircraft, include the four-digit laser code and LTL in accordance with the CAS briefing format. If aircraft check in with a different code, then it is the JTAC's responsibility to make appropriate corrections. Even if the aircraft is capable of self-designation, the JTAC should have a backup GLTD ready if it is available.

(5) **Laser Designation Time.** The aircrew may request a longer laser-on time based on munitions characteristics. If communications are unreliable, the JTAC should begin designating 20 seconds before time on target or with 20 seconds remaining on time to target (unless the aircrew is using loft delivery). Laser designation time with LGBs delivered from a loft profile will vary depending on the weapon being delivered. Refer to appropriate tactics manuals for loft laser designation time rules of thumb. While reducing laser operating time is important in a laser countermeasure environment or when using battery-operated designators, designation time must be long enough to guarantee mission success.

b. **LGW Delivery**

(1) TA is usually followed by the delivery of LGWs. Some LGWs, such as laser Maverick, and low-level LGB and/or Paveway III, can be released at ranges that may reduce the delivery aircraft's exposure to enemy air defense systems and increase aircraft survivability.

(2) Once released, the weapon homes in on reflected laser energy.

(3) Like any air delivered weapon system, the maneuver commander must fully understand and accept the consequences of a possible failure of the weapon to properly guide to the target. **The final decision to release LGWs from behind friendly lines in a laser designation operations environment rests with the maneuver commander.**

c. **Concept of Employment**

(1) **Tactical Air Control Party.** The TACP is the Marine Corps or Air Force tactical air control agency located with the supported ground unit. Its functions are providing air liaison, advising on the use of air assets, and coordinating and controlling laser designation operations missions to support the ground commander's scheme of maneuver. The TACP provides the terminal attack control of laser designation operations in support of ground forces.

(2) **Fire Support Team, Combat Observation and Lasing Team (COLT), and FO Procedures for LDO.** When possible, the LDO should be located with the FIST/COLT, and the FIST/COLT should place a radio close to the LDO (USMC LDOs may or may not be collocated with their FOs). Placing a radio close to the LDO will minimize the need to relay laser calls between the pilot and the FIST/COLT. At times, the LDO will not be with the FIST/COLT and may not be able to see the target. The LDO will coordinate laser designation with the FIST/COLT. When the LDO and FIST/COLT are not together, aircrews may make laser calls directly to the FIST/COLT on a frequency assigned by the LDO in the remarks section of the LDO briefing. In situations where the USMC LDO is not in an optimum position to designate the target, the LDO may control the aircraft with the FO actually designating the target. The USMC LDO and FO can communicate and coordinate using the TACP local net; however, prior coordination is required.

d. **Rotary Wing Procedures**

(1) **General.** Using rotary-wing aircraft to deliver LGWs allows the ground commander to destroy high-threat-point targets. Rotary-wing aircraft may be equipped with any combination of ALTDs, LSTs, and LGWs. All LTDs can assist laser-system-equipped rotary-wing aircraft in TA and provide terminal weapons guidance. Rotary-wing aircraft are employed by the Army as maneuver elements under direct control of the ground commander or aviation unit commander. One of the functions of Marine attack helicopters is to provide laser designation operations in support of the MAGTF. Precise

engagements will be aided by the use of LGWs. Army SO attack helicopter crews are also trained to perform laser designation operations with LGWs.

(2) **Laser Designation for Rotary-Wing Aircraft**

(a) **Employment.** Laser designation for TA provides fast and accurate target hand-off. Certain rotary-wing aircraft are equipped with LSTs and aid the pilot's visual TA by providing cockpit indications on the location of the laser spot. TA can be followed with the delivery of either LGWs or nonguided weapons. The aircraft can designate either for their own weapons or for other rotary-wing or fixed-wing aircraft.

(b) **Communications** between the LDO and the aircrew is essential for positive target hand-off to LST-equipped rotary-wing aircraft. Positive target hand-off requires prior coordination. The LDO must provide the appropriate laser code, LTL in degrees magnetic, and laser spot offset (if applicable).

(3) **Laser Designation for Rotary-Wing Aircraft with HELLFIRE LGMs.** The lock-on and launch ranges of LGMs can be several miles. LGMs provide extended standoff for high-threat targets. The pilot has several options for firing mode, firing method, and missile seeker lock-on.

(a) **Firing Modes**

1. **Single Fire or Manual Mode.** In the single-fire mode, one missile is launched. This mode can be used with autonomous direct, remote direct, and remote indirect fire methods, as discussed below.

2. **Rapid Fire.** Rapid fire is a technique of launching two or more missiles on the same code. Multiple targets can be engaged by launching missiles at least 8 seconds or more apart, as specified by the LDO. Once the first missile hits the first target, the LDO must smoothly move the laser spot to the next target.

3. **Ripple Fire.** In the ripple fire mode, missiles are fired one after the other on different codes. For best effect, multiple LTDs should be used to achieve ripple fire. Each LTD operates on a different laser code, and the weapon's seekers are coded to match each designator.

4. **Rapid or Ripple Fire.** Using multiple codes and LTDs, the combination of rapid or ripple fire can be achieved.

(b) **Firing Methods**

1. **Direct Fire Method.** Direct fire is achieved using either autonomous or remote LTDs. When using remote designators, the rotary-wing aircraft is free to resume terrain masking or engage other targets after each LGM launch. This capability is called "fire and forget" and increases aircraft survivability and flexibility.

2. **Indirect Fire Method.** Indirect fire is achieved by using remote LTDs. Vulnerability of rotary-wing aircraft to enemy direct-fire weapons and radar detection is minimized by employing LGMs in the indirect-fire method. The LGM is launched while the aircraft is positioned behind masking terrain features, like trees and hills. The pilot selects a trajectory for the LGM (either high or low) over the masking terrain feature. The seeker will then locate and lock on to the remote laser-designated target.

(c) HELLFIRE Missile Seeker Lock-on Options

<u>1.</u> **Lock-on After Launch.** The LOAL option can be used in the direct-fire mode and is always used for the indirect-fire method. The LGM is launched on a trajectory toward the target with seeker lock-on occurring in flight. This option allows missile launching toward the target area during adverse weather, hazy days, long ranges, or temporary target obscuration. Lock-on will occur when the obstruction to the seeker's view dissipates or is bypassed during the approach to the target area.

<u>2.</u> **Lock-on Before Launch.** The LOBL option requires direct LOS to the target and requires the seeker to be locked on to the target before launch.

(d) **Fratricide.** To keep the Hellfire missile from locking onto the designator instead of the target, Angle-T between the designator-target line and the missile target line should be less than 1,065 mils (60 degrees). The LDO must ensure the launch platform operator knows the location of the observer so that the launch platform can be repositioned if necessary for safety.

For additional information on the Army FA laser operations, see FM 6-30, TTP for Observed Fire.

See FM 3-09.32/MCRP 3-16.6A/NTTP 3-09.2/AFTTP(I) 3-2.6, JFIRE, Multi-Service Tactics, Techniques, and Procedures for the Joint Application of Firepower, *for additional information on laser operations.*

See JP 3-09.3, Close Air Support, *for expanded discussion of laser-guided considerations for CAS.*

APPENDIX D
REFERENCES

The development of JP 3-09 is based upon the following primary references:

1. DOD Publications

    a. CJCSI 3121.01B, *Standing Rules of Engagement/Standing Rules for the Use of Force for US Forces.*

    b. CJCSI 3160.01, *No-Strike and the Collateral Damage Estimation Methodology.*

    c. CJCSI 3505.01, *Target Coordinate Mensuration Certification and Program Accreditation.*

    d. CJCSI 3900.01 Series, *Position Reference Procedures.*

    e. JP 1, *Doctrine for the Armed Forces of the United States.*

    f. JP 2-0, *Joint Intelligence.*

    g. JP 2-01, *Joint and National Intelligence Support to Military Operations.*

    h. JP 2-03, *Geospatial Intelligence Support to Joint Operations.*

    i. JP 3-0, *Joint Operations.*

    j. JP 3-01, *Countering Air and Missile Threats.*

    k. JP 3-02, *Amphibious Operations.*

    l. JP 3-03, *Joint Interdiction.*

    m. JP 3-05, *Joint Special Operations.*

    n. JP 3-09.3, *Close Air Support.*

    o. JP 3-13, *Information Operations.*

    p. JP 3-13.1, *Electronic Warfare.*

    q. JP 3-16, *Multinational Operations.*

    r. JP 3-30, *Command and Control for Joint Air Operations.*

    s. JP 3-33, *Joint Task Force Headquarters.*

t. JP 3-52, *Joint Airspace Control.*

u. JP 3-60, *Joint Targeting.*

v. JP 6-0, *Joint Communications System.*

2. Multi-Service Publications

a. FM 3-01.20/AFTTP(I) 3-2.30, *Multi-Service Tactics, Techniques, and Procedures for JAOC/AAMDC Coordination.*

b. FM 3-09.32/MCRP 3-16.6B/NTTP 3-09.2/AFTTP(I) 3-2.6, *JFIRE, Multi-Service Procedures for the Joint Application of Firepower.*

c. FM 3-09.34/MCRP 3-25H/NTTP 3-09.2.1/AFTTP(I) 3-2.59, *KILL BOX, Multi-Service Tactics, Techniques, and Procedures for Kill Box Employment.*

3. Service Publication

FM 6-30, *Tactics, Techniques, and Procedures for Observed Fire.*

4. Combatant Command Publications

a. USJFCOM Joint Fires and Targeting Handbook.

b. USSTRATCOM Global Strike Plan and Emergency Action Procedures.

APPENDIX E
ADMINISTRATIVE INSTRUCTIONS

1. User Comments

Users in the field are highly encouraged to submit comments on this publication to: CDR, USJFCOM, Joint Warfighting Center, ATTN: Doctrine and Education Group, 116 Lake View Parkway, Suffolk, VA 23435-2697. These comments should address content (accuracy, usefulness, consistency, and organization), writing, and appearance.

2. Authorship

The lead agent for this publication is USJFCOM. The Joint Staff doctrine sponsor for this publication is the Director for Strategic Plans and Policy (J-5).

3. Supersession

This publication supersedes JP 3-09, *Joint Fire Support,* 13 November 2006. JP 3-09.1, *Joint Tactics, Techniques, and Procedures for Laser Designation Operations,* dated 28 May 1999, is cancelled.

4. Change Recommendations

a. Recommendations for urgent changes to this publication should be submitted:

    TO: CDRUSJFCOM SUFFOLK VA//DOC GP//
    INFO: JOINT STAFF WASHINGTON DC//J7-JEDD//

Routine changes should be submitted electronically to CDR, Joint Warfighting Center, Doctrine and Education Group and info Director for Operational Plans and Joint Force Development J-7/JEDD via the CJCS JEL at http://www.dtic.mil/doctrine.

b. When a Joint Staff directorate submits a proposal to the CJCS that would change source document information reflected in this publication, that directorate will include a proposed change to this publication as an enclosure to its proposal. The Military Services and other organizations are requested to notify the Joint Staff J-7, when changes to source documents reflected in this publication are initiated.

c. Record of Changes:

CHANGE NUMBER	COPY NUMBER	DATE OF CHANGE	DATE ENTERED	POSTED BY	REMARKS

5. Distribution of Publications

Local reproduction is authorized and access to unclassified publications is unrestricted. However, access to and reproduction authorization for classified JPs must be in accordance with DOD 5200.1-R, *Information Security Program.*

6. Distribution of Electronic Publications

a. The Joint Staff will not print copies of electronic JPs for distribution. Electronic versions are available on JDEIS at https://jdeis.js.mil (NIPRNET) and https://jdeis.js.smil.mil (SIPRNET), and on the JEL at http://www.dtic.mil/doctrine (NIPRNET).

b. Only approved JPs and joint test publications are releasable outside the combatant commands, Services, and Joint Staff. Release of any classified JP to foreign governments or foreign nationals must be requested through the local embassy (Defense Attaché Office) to DIA, Defense Foreign Liaison/IE-3, 200 MacDill Blvd., Bolling AFB, Washington, DC 20340-5100.

c. CD-ROM. Upon request of a joint doctrine development community member, the Joint Staff J-7 will produce and deliver one CD-ROM with current JPs.

GLOSSARY
PART I — ABBREVIATIONS AND ACRONYMS

AADC	area air defense commander
AAMDC	US Army Air and Missile Defense Command
ABP	air battle plan
ACA	airspace coordination area
ACE	aviation combat element (MAGTF)
ACM	airspace coordinating measure
ACO	airspace control order
AFATDS	Advanced Field Artillery Tactical Data System
AFTTP(I)	Air Force tactics, techniques, and procedures (instruction)
AGL	above ground level
AI	air interdiction
ALTD	airborne laser target designator
AO	area of operations
AOA	amphibious objective area
AOC	air and space operations center (USAF)
ARFOR	Army forces
ASOC	air support operations center
ATACMS	Army Tactical Missile System
ATCS	air traffic control section
ATF	amphibious task force
ATO	air tasking order
AWACS	Airborne Warning and Control System
BCD	battlefield coordination detachment
C2	command and control
CA	combat assessment
CALCM	conventional air-launched cruise missile
CAS	close air support
CATF	commander, amphibious task force
CC	critical capability
CDE	collateral damage estimation
CDRJSOTF	commander, joint special operations task force
CENTRIXS	Combined Enterprise Regional Information Exchange System
CF-COP	counterfire common operational picture
CFL	coordinated fire line
CID	combat identification
CJCSI	Chairman of the Joint Chiefs of Staff instruction
CLF	commander, landing force
CNA	computer network attack
COA	course of action
COF	chief of fires
COG	center of gravity
COLT	combat observation and lasing team

CONOPS	concept of operations
CRC	control and reporting center
CSW	coordinate seeking weapons
DASC	direct air support center
DOD	Department of Defense
DS	direct support
DTG	date-time group
EA	electronic attack
EM	electromagnetic
EW	electronic warfare
EZM	engagement zone manager
FA	field artillery
FAC(A)	forward air controller (airborne)
FFA	free-fire area
FFCC	force fires coordination center
FIST	fire support team
FLOT	forward line of own troops
FM	field manual (Army)
FO	forward observer
FSA	fire support area
FSC	fire support coordinator (USMC)
FSCC	fire support coordination center
FSCL	fire support coordination line
FSCM	fire support coordination measure
FSO	fire support officer
FSS	fire support station
ft	feet
GARS	Global Area Reference System
GCE	ground combat element (MAGTF)
GLTD	ground laser target designator
GPS	Global Positioning System
GS	general support
HIMARS	High Mobility Artillery Rocket System
HPT	high-payoff target
HQ	headquarters
HVT	high-value target

IGO	intergovernmental organization
IO	information operations
ISR	intelligence, surveillance, and reconnaissance
J-3	operations directorate of a joint staff
JACCE	joint air component coordination element
JADOCS	Joint Automated Deep Operations Coordination System
JAOC	joint air operations center
JASSM	joint air-to-surface standoff missile
JFACC	joint force air component commander
JFC	joint force commander
JFE	joint fires element
JFLCC	joint force land component commander
JFO	joint fires observer
JFSOCC	joint force special operations component commander
JIPTL	joint integrated prioritized target list
JOA	joint operations area
JP	joint publication
JPG	joint planning group
JSCP	Joint Strategic Capabilities Plan
J-SEAD	joint suppression of enemy air defenses
JSOA	joint special operations area
JSOACC	joint special operations air component commander
JSOTF	joint special operations task force
JSTARS	Joint Surveillance Target Attack Radar System
JTAC	joint terminal attack controller
JTCB	joint targeting coordination board
JTF	joint task force
LDO	laser designator operator
LF	landing force
LGB	laser-guided bomb
LGM	laser-guided missile
LGW	laser-guided weapon
LO	low observable
LOAL	lock-on after launch
LOBL	lock-on before launch
LOC	line of communications
LOS	line of sight
LRF	laser rangefinder
LST	laser spot tracker
LTD	laser target designator
LTL	laser-to-target line
MACCS	Marine air command and control system
MAGTF	Marine air-ground task force
MCRP	Marine Corps reference publication

MEF	Marine expeditionary force
MIDB	modernized integrated database
MLRS	Multiple Launch Rocket System
NATO	North Atlantic Treaty Organization
NCO	noncommissioned officer
NFA	no-fire area
NGO	nongovernmental organization
NIPRNET	Non-Secure Internet Protocol Router Network
NSFS	naval surface fire support
NSL	no-strike list
NSWTG	naval special warfare task group
NSWTU	naval special warfare task unit
NTTP	Navy tactics, techniques, and procedures
OGA	other government agency
OPCON	operational control
OPLAN	operation plan
OPORD	operation order
PL	phase line
PRF	pulse repetition frequency
RFA	restrictive fire area
RFL	restrictive fire line
ROE	rules of engagement
RTL	restricted target list
SA	situational awareness
SACC	supporting arms coordination center
SFCP	shore fire control party
SIPRNET	SECRET Internet Protocol Router Network
SO	special operations
SOCCE	special operations command and control element
SOCOORD	special operations coordination element
SOF	special operations forces
SOLE	special operations liaison element
SOP	standard operating procedure
STANAG	standardization agreement (NATO)
STT	special tactics team
TA	target acquisition
TAC(A)	tactical air coordinator (airborne)
TACC	tactical air command center (USMC); tactical air control center (USN)
TACP	tactical air control party
TADC	tactical air direction center

TAMD	theater air and missile defense
TAOC	tactical air operations center (USMC)
TBMCS	theater battle management core system
TGO	terminal guidance operations
TLAM	Tomahawk land attack missile
TLE	target location error
TM	theater missile
TST	time-sensitive target
UAS	unmanned aircraft system
USJFCOM	United States Joint Forces Command
USMC	United States Marine Corps
USSTRATCOM	United States Strategic Command
WMD	weapons of mass destruction
ZF	zone of fire

Unless otherwise annotated, this publication is the proponent for all terms and definitions found in the glossary. Upon approval, JP 1-02, *Department of Defense Dictionary of Military and Associated Terms*, will reflect this publication as the source document for these terms and definitions.

air interdiction. Air operations conducted to divert, disrupt, delay, or destroy the enemy's military potential before it can be brought to bear effectively against friendly forces, or to otherwise achieve objectives. Air interdiction is conducted at such distance from friendly forces that detailed integration of each air mission with the fire and movement of friendly forces is not required. (JP 1-02. SOURCE: JP 3-0)

airspace control authority. The commander designated to assume overall responsibility for the operation of the airspace control system in the airspace control area. Also called **ACA.** (JP 1-02. SOURCE: JP 3-52)

airspace coordinating measures. Measures employed to facilitate the efficient use of airspace to accomplish missions and simultaneously provide safeguards for friendly forces. Also called **ACMs.** (JP 1-02. SOURCE: JP 3-52)

airspace coordination area. A three-dimensional block of airspace in a target area, established by the appropriate ground commander, in which friendly aircraft are reasonably safe from friendly surface fires. The airspace coordination area may be formal or informal. Also called **ACA.** (JP 1-02. SOURCE: JP 3-09.3)

air tasking order. A method used to task and disseminate to components, subordinate units, and command and control agencies projected sorties, capabilities and/or forces to targets and specific missions. Normally provides specific instructions to include call signs, targets, controlling agencies, etc., as well as general instructions. Also called **ATO.** (JP 1-02. SOURCE: JP 3-30)

area of operations. An operational area defined by the joint force commander for land and maritime forces. Areas of operation do not typically encompass the entire operational area of the joint force commander, but should be large enough for component commanders to accomplish their missions and protect their forces. Also called **AO.** (JP 1-02. SOURCE: JP 3-0)

at my command. None. (Approved for removal from JP 1-02.)

backscatter. None. (Approved for removal from JP 1-02.)

boundary. A line that delineates surface areas for the purpose of facilitating coordination and deconfliction of operations between adjacent units, formations, or areas. (JP 1-02. SOURCE: JP 3-0)

call fire. None. (Approved for removal from JP 1-02.)

call for fire. None. (Approved for removal from JP 1-02.)

center of gravity. The source of power that provides moral or physical strength, freedom of action, or will to act. Also called **COG.** (JP 1-02. SOURCE: JP 3-0)

close air support. Air action by fixed- and rotary-wing aircraft against hostile targets that are in close proximity to friendly forces and that require detailed integration of each air mission with the fire and movement of those forces. Also called **CAS.** (JP 1-02. SOURCE: 3-0)

collateral damage. Unintentional or incidental injury or damage to persons or objects that would not be lawful military targets in the circumstances ruling at the time. Such damage is not unlawful so long as it is not excessive in light of the overall military advantage anticipated from the attack. (JP 1-02. SOURCE: JP 3-60)

combat identification. The process of attaining an accurate characterization of detected objects in the operational environment sufficient to support an engagement decision. Also called **CID.** (JP 1-02. SOURCE: JP 3-09)

computer network operations. Comprised of computer network attack, computer network defense, and related computer network exploitation enabling operations. Also called **CNO.** (JP 1-02. SOURCE: 3-13)

concept of fires. A verbal or graphic statement that clearly and concisely expresses how lethal and nonlethal fires will be synchronized and integrated to support the commander's operational objectives. (Approved for inclusion in JP 1-02.)

concept of operations. A verbal or graphic statement, that clearly and concisely expresses what the joint force commander intends to accomplish and how it will be done using available resources. The concept is designed to give an overall picture of the operation. Also called **commander's concept** or **CONOPS.** (JP 1-02. SOURCE: JP 5-0)

continuous illumination fire. None. (Approved for removal from JP 1-02.)

coordinated fire line. A line beyond which conventional and indirect surface fire support means may fire at any time within the boundaries of the establishing headquarters without additional coordination. The purpose of the coordinated fire line is to expedite the surface-to-surface attack of targets beyond the coordinated fire line without coordination with the ground commander in whose area the targets are located. Also called **CFL.** (JP 1-02. SOURCE: JP 3-09)

counterfire. Fire intended to destroy or neutralize enemy weapons. Includes counterbattery and countermortar fire. (Approved for incorporation into JP 1-02.)

defilade. 1. Protection from hostile observation and fire provided by an obstacle such as a hill, ridge, or bank. 2. A vertical distance by which a position is concealed from enemy observation. 3. To shield from enemy fire or observation by using natural or artificial obstacles. (Approved for incorporation into JP 1-02 with JP 3-09 as the source JP.)

directed energy. An umbrella term covering technologies that relate to the production of a beam of concentrated electromagnetic energy or atomic or subatomic particles. Also called **DE.** (Approved for incorporation into JP 1-02 with JP 3-09 as the source JP.)

direct support artillery. None. (Approved for removal from JP 1-02.)

electronic attack. Division of electronic warfare involving the use of electromagnetic energy, directed energy, or antiradiation weapons to attack personnel, facilities, or equipment with the intent of degrading, neutralizing, or destroying enemy combat capability and is considered a form of fires. Also called **EA.** (JP 1-02. SOURCE: JP 3-13.1)

electronic warfare. Military action involving the use of electromagnetic and directed energy to control the electromagnetic spectrum or to attack the enemy. Electronic warfare consists of three divisions: electronic attack, electronic protection, and electronic warfare support. Also called **EW.** (JP 1-02. SOURCE: JP 3-13.1)

enlisted terminal attack controller. None. (Approved for removal from JP 1-02.)

field artillery. Equipment, supplies, ammunition, and personnel involved in the use of cannon, rocket, or surface-to-surface missile launchers. Field artillery cannons are classified according to caliber as follows:
Light — 120mm and less.
Medium — 121-160mm.
Heavy — 161-210mm.
Very heavy — greater than 210mm.
Also called **FA.** (Approved for incorporation into JP 1-02 with JP 3-09 as the source JP.)

fire. None. (Approved for removal from JP 1-02.)

fire barrage (specify). None. (Approved for removal from JP 1-02.)

fire capabilities chart. None. (Approved for removal from JP 1-02.)

fire control. None. (Approved for removal from JP 1-02.)

fire control radar. None. (Approved for removal from JP 1-02.)

fire control system. None. (Approved for removal from JP 1-02.)

fire coordination. None. (Approved for removal from JP 1-02.)

fire for effect. None. (Approved for removal from JP 1-02.)

fire message. None. (Approved for removal from JP 1-02.)

fire mission. None. (Approved for removal from JP 1-02.)

fire plan. None. (Approved for removal from JP 1-02.)

firepower. None. (Approved for removal from JP 1-02.)

fires. The use of weapon systems to create specific lethal or nonlethal effects on a target. (Approved for incorporation into JP 1-02.)

fire support. Fires that directly support land, maritime, amphibious, and special operations forces to engage enemy forces, combat formations, and facilities in pursuit of tactical and operational objectives. (JP 1-02. SOURCE: JP 3-09)

fire support area. An appropriate maneuver area assigned to fire support ships by the naval force commander from which they can deliver gunfire support to an amphibious operation. Also called **FSA.** (JP 1-02. SOURCE: JP 3-09)

fire support coordination. The planning and executing of fire so that targets are adequately covered by a suitable weapon or group of weapons. (JP 1-02. SOURCE: JP 3-09)

fire support coordination center. A single location in which are centralized communications facilities and personnel incident to the coordination of all forms of fire support. Also called **FSCC.** (Approved for incorporation into JP 1-02 with JP 3-09 as the source JP.)

fire support coordination line. A fire support coordination measure that is established and adjusted by appropriate land or amphibious force commanders within their boundaries in consultation with superior, subordinate, supporting, and affected commanders. Fire support coordination lines facilitate the expeditious attack of surface targets of opportunity beyond the coordinating measure. A fire support coordination line does not divide an area of operations by defining a boundary between close and deep operations or a zone for close air support. The fire support coordination line applies to all fires of air, land, and sea-based weapon systems using any type of ammunition. Forces attacking targets beyond a fire support coordination line must inform all affected commanders in sufficient time to allow necessary reaction to avoid fratricide. Supporting elements attacking targets beyond the fire support coordination line must ensure that the attack will not produce adverse effects on, or to the rear of, the line. Short of a fire support coordination line, all air-to-ground and surface-to-surface attack operations are controlled by the appropriate land or amphibious force commander. The fire support coordination line should follow well-defined terrain features. Coordination of attacks beyond the fire support coordination line is especially critical to commanders of air, land, and special operations forces. In exceptional circumstances, the inability to conduct this coordination will not preclude the attack of targets beyond the fire support coordination line. However, failure to do so may increase the risk of fratricide and could waste limited resources. Also called **FSCL.** (JP 1-02. SOURCE: JP 3-09)

fire support coordination measure. A measure employed by land or amphibious commanders to facilitate the rapid engagement of targets and simultaneously provide safeguards for friendly forces. Also called **FSCM.** (JP 1-02. SOURCE: JP 3-0)

fire support element. That portion of the force tactical operations center at every echelon above company or troop (to corps) that is responsible for targeting coordination and for integrating fires delivered on surface targets by fire-support means under the control, or in support, of the force. Also called **FSE.** (JP 1-02. SOURCE: JP 3-09)

fire support officer. Senior field artillery officer assigned to Army maneuver battalions and brigades. Advises commander on fire-support matters. Also called **FSO.** (Approved for incorporation into JP 1-02 with JP 3-09 as the source JP.)

fire support station. An exact location at sea within a fire support area from which a fire support ship delivers fire. Also called **FSS.** (JP 1-02. SOURCE: JP 3-02)

firing chart. None. (Approved for removal from JP 1-02.)

forward observer. An observer operating with front line troops and trained to adjust ground or naval gunfire and pass back battlefield information. In the absence of a forward air controller, the observer may control close air support strikes. Also called **FO.** (Approved for incorporation into JP 1-02 with JP 3-09 as the source JP.)

free-fire area. A specific area into which any weapon system may fire without additional coordination with the establishing headquarters. Also called **FFA.** (JP 1-02. SOURCE: JP 3-09)

grid coordinates. Coordinates of a grid coordinate system to which numbers and letters are assigned for use in designating a point on a gridded map, photograph, or chart. (JP 1-02. SOURCE: JP 3-09)

high-payoff target. A target whose loss to the enemy will significantly contribute to the success of the friendly course of action. High-payoff targets are those high-value targets that must be acquired and successfully attacked for the success of the friendly commander's mission. Also called **HPT**. (JP 1-02. SOURCE: JP 3-60)

high-value target. A target the enemy commander requires for the successful completion of the mission. The loss of high-value targets would be expected to seriously degrade important enemy functions throughout the friendly commander's area of interest. Also called **HVT**. (JP 1-02. SOURCE: JP 3-60)

inertial navigation system. A self-contained navigation system using inertial detectors, which automatically provides vehicle position, heading, and velocity. Also called **INS**. (JP 1-02. SOURCE: JP 3-09)

interdiction. 1. An action to divert, disrupt, delay, or destroy the enemy's military surface capability before it can be used effectively against friendly forces, or to otherwise achieve objectives. 2. In support of law enforcement, activities conducted to divert, disrupt, delay, intercept, board, detain, or destroy, as appropriate, vessels, vehicles, aircraft, people, and cargo. (JP 1-02. SOURCE: JP 3-03)

joint fires. Fires delivered during the employment of forces from two or more components in coordinated action to produce desired effects in support of a common objective. (JP 1-02. SOURCE: JP 3-0)

joint fires element. An optional staff element that provides recommendations to the operations directorate to accomplish fires planning and synchronization. Also called **JFE**. (JP 1-02. SOURCE: JP 3-60)

joint fire support. Joint fires that assist air, land, maritime, and special operations forces to move, maneuver, and control territory, populations, airspace, and key waters. (JP 1-02. SOURCE: JP 3-0)

joint force air component commander. The commander within a unified command, subordinate unified command, or joint task force responsible to the establishing commander for making recommendations on the proper employment of assigned, attached, and/or made available for tasking air forces; planning and coordinating air operations; or accomplishing such operational missions as may be assigned. The joint force air component commander is given the authority necessary to accomplish missions and tasks assigned by the establishing commander. Also called **JFACC**. (JP 1-02. SOURCE: JP 3-0)

joint targeting coordination board. A group formed by the joint force commander to accomplish broad targeting oversight functions that may include but are not limited to coordinating targeting information, providing targeting guidance and priorities, and refining the joint integrated prioritized target list. The board is normally comprised of representatives from the joint force staff, all components, and if required, component subordinate units. Also called **JTCB**. (JP 1-02. SOURCE: JP 3-60)

kill box. A three-dimensional area used to facilitate the integration of joint fires. (JP 1-02. SOURCE: JP 3-09)

laser. None. (Approved for removal from JP 1-02.)

laser footprint. None. (Approved for removal from JP 1-02.)

laser guided weapon. A weapon which uses a seeker to detect laser energy reflected from a laser marked/designated target and through signal processing provides guidance commands to a control system which guides the weapon to the point from which the laser energy is being reflected. Also called **LGW.** (JP 1-02. SOURCE: JP 3-09)

laser linescan system. None. (Approved for removal from JP 1-02.)

laser pulse duration. None. (Approved for removal from JP 1-02.)

laser rangefinder. A device which uses laser energy for determining the distance from the device to a place or object. (JP 1-02. SOURCE: JP 3-09)

laser seeker. A device based on a direction sensitive receiver which detects the energy reflected from a laser designated target and defines the direction of the target relative to the receiver. (JP 1-02. SOURCE: JP 3-09)

laser spot. The area on a surface illuminated by a laser. (Approved for incorporation into JP 1-02 with JP 3-09 as the source JP.)

laser spot tracker. A device that locks on to the reflected energy from a laser-marked or designated target and defines the direction of the target relative to itself. Also called **LST.** (Approved for incorporation into JP 1-02 with JP 3-09 as the source JP.)

laser target designating system. None. (Approved for removal from JP 1-02.)

laser target designator. A device that emits a beam of laser energy which is used to mark a specific place or object. Also called **LTD.** (Approved for incorporation into JP 1-02 with JP 3-09 as the source JP.)

laser-target/gun-target angle. None. (Approved for removal from JP 1-02.)

laser target marker. None. (Approved for removal from JP 1-02.)

laser target marking system. None. (Approved for removal from JP 1-02.)

low angle. None. (Approved for removal from JP 1-02.)

low angle fire. None. (Approved for removal from JP 1-02.)

low angle loft bombing. None. (Approved for removal from JP 1-02.)

mensuration. The process of measurement of a feature or location on the earth to determine an absolute latitude, longitude, and elevation. For targeting applications, the errors inherent in both the source for measurement as well as the measurement processes must be understood and reported. (JP 1-02. SOURCE: JP 3-60)

no-fire area. An area designated by the appropriate commander into which fires or their effects are prohibited. Also called **NFA.** (JP 1-02. SOURCE: JP 3-09.3)

nonlethal weapon. A weapon that is explicitly designed and primarily employed so as to incapacitate personnel or materiel, while minimizing fatalities, permanent injury to personnel, and undesired damage to property and the environment. Also called **NLW.** (1-02. SOURCE: JP 3-28)

no-strike list. A list of objects or entities characterized as protected from the effects of military operations under international law and/or rules of engagement. Attacking these may violate the law of armed conflict or interfere with friendly relations with indigenous personnel or governments. Also called **NSL.** (JP 1-02. SOURCE: JP 3-60)

offset lasing. None. (Approved for removal from JP 1-02.)

phase line. A line utilized for control and coordination of military operations, usually an easily identified feature in the operational area. Also called **PL.** (1-02. SOURCE: JP 3-09)

positive control. A method of airspace control that relies on positive identification, tracking, and direction of aircraft within an airspace, conducted with electronic means by an agency having the authority and responsibility therein. (JP 1-02. SOURCE: 3-52)

prearranged fire. Fire that is formally planned and executed against targets or target areas of known location. Such fire is usually planned well in advance and is executed at a predetermined time or during a predetermined period of time. (JP 1-02. SOURCE: JP 3-09)

procedural control. A method of airspace control which relies on a combination of previously agreed and promulgated orders and procedures. (JP 1-02. SOURCE: JP 3-52)

pulse code. None. (Approved for removal from JP 1-02.)

pulse repetition frequency. None. (Approved for removal from JP 1-02.)

rate of fire. None. (Approved for removal from JP 1-02.)

restrictive fire area. An area in which specific restrictions are imposed and into which fires that exceed those restrictions will not be delivered without coordination with the establishing headquarters. Also called **RFA.** (JP 1-02. SOURCE: JP 3-09)

restrictive fire line. A line established between converging friendly surface forces that prohibits fires or their effects across that line. Also called **RFL.** (JP 1-02. SOURCE: JP 3-09)

rules of engagement. Directives issued by competent military authority that delineate the circumstances and limitations under which United States forces will initiate and/or continue combat engagement with other forces encountered. Also called **ROE.** (JP 1-02. SOURCE: JP 1-04)

schedule of fire. Groups of fires or series of fires fired in a definite sequence according to a definite program. The time of starting the schedule may be on call. For identification purposes, schedules may be referred to by a code name or other designation. (Approved for incorporation into JP 1-02.)

special operations terminal attack controller. None. (Approved for removal from JP 1-02.)

spillover. None. (Approved for removal from JP 1-02.)

submunition. None. (Approved for removal from JP 1-02.)

supporting fire. Fire delivered by supporting units to assist or protect a unit in combat. (Approved for incorporation into JP 1-02 with JP 3-09 as the source JP.)

targeting. The process of selecting and prioritizing targets and matching the appropriate response to them, considering operational requirements and capabilities. (JP 1-02. SOURCE: JP 3-0)

target of opportunity. 1. A target identified too late, or not selected for action in time, to be included in deliberate targeting that, when detected or located, meets criteria specific to achieving objectives and is processed using dynamic targeting. There are two types of targets of opportunity: unplanned and unanticipated. 2. A target visible to a surface or air sensor or observer, which is within range of available weapons and against which fire has not been scheduled or requested. (JP 1-02. SOURCE: JP 3-60)

terminal guidance operations. Those actions that provide electronic, mechanical, voice or visual communications that provide approaching aircraft and/or weapons additional information regarding a specific target location. Also called **TGO.** (JP 1-02. SOURCE: JP 3-09)

time-sensitive target. A joint force commander designated target requiring immediate response because it is a highly lucrative, fleeting target of opportunity or it poses (or will soon pose) a danger to friendly forces. Also called **TST.** (JP 1-02. SOURCE: JP 3-60)

zone of action. A tactical subdivision of a larger area, the responsibility for which is assigned to a tactical unit; generally applied to offensive action. (JP 1-02. SOURCE: JP 3-09.)

zone of fire. An area into which a designated ground unit or fire support ship delivers, or is prepared to deliver, fire support. Fire may or may not be observed. Also called **ZF.** (JP 1-02. SOURCE: JP 3-09)

Intentionally Blank

JOINT DOCTRINE PUBLICATIONS HIERARCHY

```
                        ┌──────────────┐
                        │    JP 1      │
                        │   JOINT      │
                        │  DOCTRINE    │
                        └──────┬───────┘
    ┌──────────┬──────────┬────┴─────┬──────────┬──────────┐
┌────────┐ ┌──────────┐ ┌────────┐ ┌────────┐ ┌────────┐ ┌──────────────┐
│ JP 1-0 │ │  JP 2-0  │ │ JP 3-0 │ │ JP 4-0 │ │ JP 5-0 │ │   JP 6-0     │
│PERSONNEL│ │INTELLIGENCE│ │OPERATIONS│ │LOGISTICS│ │ PLANS │ │COMMUNICATION│
│         │ │          │ │        │ │        │ │        │ │   SYSTEMS    │
└────────┘ └──────────┘ └────────┘ └────────┘ └────────┘ └──────────────┘
```

All joint publications are organized into a comprehensive hierarchy as shown in the chart above. **Joint Publication (JP) 3-09** is in the **Operations** series of joint doctrine publications. The diagram below illustrates an overview of the development process:

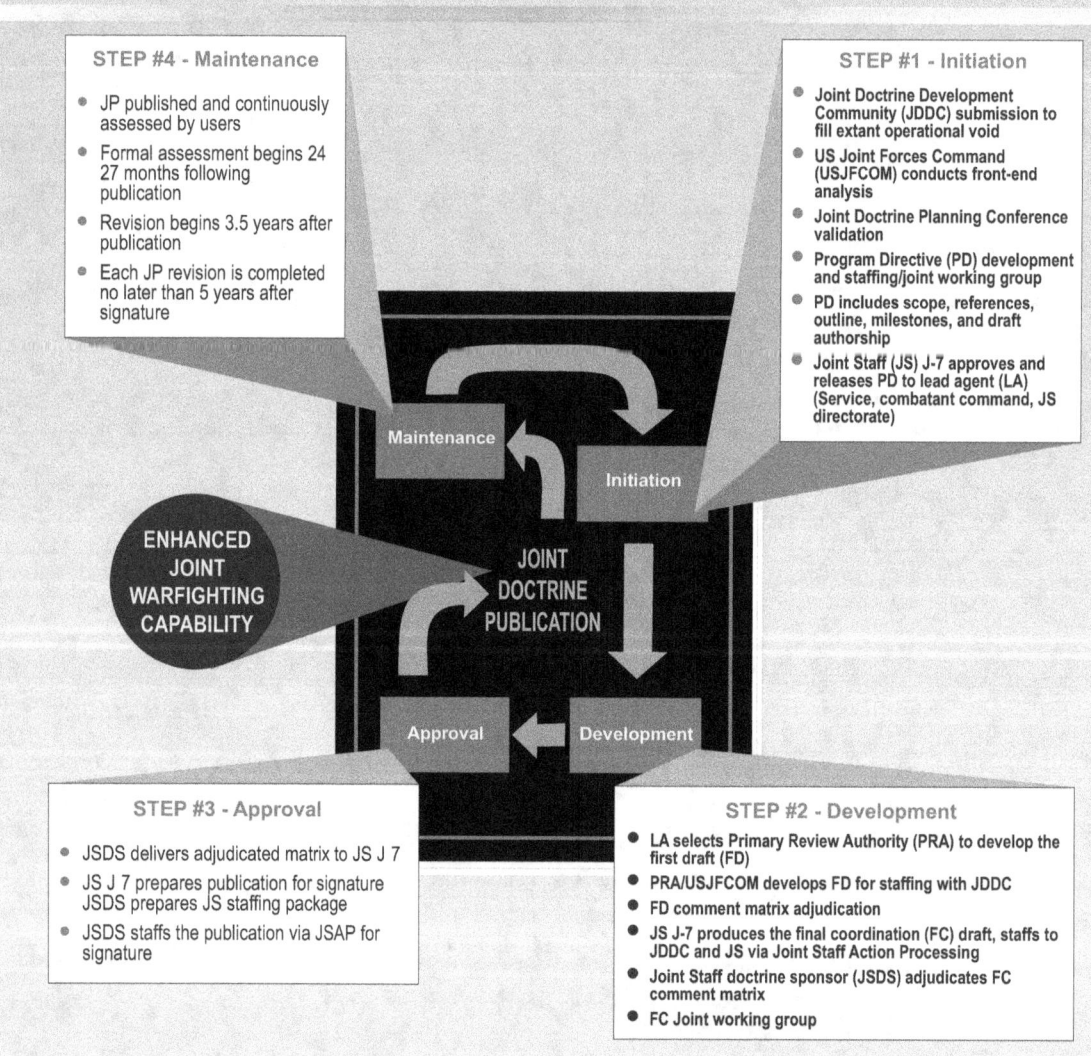

STEP #4 - Maintenance

- JP published and continuously assessed by users
- Formal assessment begins 24 27 months following publication
- Revision begins 3.5 years after publication
- Each JP revision is completed no later than 5 years after signature

STEP #1 - Initiation

- Joint Doctrine Development Community (JDDC) submission to fill extant operational void
- US Joint Forces Command (USJFCOM) conducts front-end analysis
- Joint Doctrine Planning Conference validation
- Program Directive (PD) development and staffing/joint working group
- PD includes scope, references, outline, milestones, and draft authorship
- Joint Staff (JS) J-7 approves and releases PD to lead agent (LA) (Service, combatant command, JS directorate)

STEP #3 - Approval

- JSDS delivers adjudicated matrix to JS J 7
- JS J 7 prepares publication for signature JSDS prepares JS staffing package
- JSDS staffs the publication via JSAP for signature

STEP #2 - Development

- LA selects Primary Review Authority (PRA) to develop the first draft (FD)
- PRA/USJFCOM develops FD for staffing with JDDC
- FD comment matrix adjudication
- JS J-7 produces the final coordination (FC) draft, staffs to JDDC and JS via Joint Staff Action Processing
- Joint Staff doctrine sponsor (JSDS) adjudicates FC comment matrix
- FC Joint working group

www.ingramcontent.com/pod-product-compliance
Lightning Source LLC
Chambersburg PA
CBHW081327310526

45789CB00018B/2459